With Confidence

With Confidence

Your Life Your Way

RIKY ASH

THE CHOIR PRESS

Copyright © 2026 Riky Ash

All rights reserved. No part of this publication may be reproduced or transmitted in any form or by any means, electronic or mechanical including photocopying, recording or any information storage or retrieval system, without prior permission in writing from the publishers.

The right of Riky Ash to be identified as the author of this work has been asserted by him in accordance with the Copyright, Designs and Patents Act 1988

First published in the United Kingdom in 2026 by
The Choir Press

ISBN 978-1-78963-508-9

Contents

Why? vii

Introduction ix

Words Of Wisdom xi

Chapter 1 - My Story of Success 1

Chapter 2 - Controlling the Uncontrollable 14

Chapter 3 - A Disciplined Mind 24

Chapter 4 - Motivation 38

Chapter 5 - Mixing With the Right Kind of People 54

Chapter 6 - Turning a Negative Experience into a Positive One 66

Chapter 7 - There is More than one Pebble on the Beach 75

Chapter 8 - Communication 82

Chapter 9 - Develop a Positive Attitude towards your Life 93

Chapter 10 - Achieving Goals 105

Chapter 11 - Become More Assertive Within Yourself 119

Chapter 12 - Welcome to the Real World 129

Chapter 13 - Creating your own Happiness 149

Chapter 14 - Dressed for Success 161

End

Why?

I first wrote this book in 2005; it was then published in 2006. What inspired me to write such a book was that I regularly gave out no-nonsense information to help people become confident and successful and, as what I say works, a friend was so inspired he suggested I write a book.

I created quite a following long before social media even existed. I was new to publishing and through inexperience I wrongly chose an American publishing house which resulted in various problems. I removed With Confidence from circulation, keeping just one copy for myself.

My then doctor, Kevin, who is now one of my closest friends, borrowed my book for his wife to help her with some confidence issues she was having. She was able to obtain near-instant results from putting my words into practice. This prompted me to do one of two things – firstly, I would rewrite my book, although this time in a much harder and more direct format. No more Mr Nice Guy, the reason being that I have changed, and the world has changed so much for the worse, our appalling government trying to control us. I had established that I attributed my amazing success to my unique personality.

I simply do things differently and I always get positive results, that is how I am. I do not obey the laws of the land, why should I? In my very good friend Roger's words, they are fucked up anyway. I create my own Set of Rules for life.

I do not do political correctness; I cannot be tamed, I cannot be controlled, most of what I learned at school was just pointless. From the very young age of 19 I was able to work the government out, that they do not care about you or me, they only care about themselves. They need you and I to be their slaves, they need you and I to be subservient and controlled. Work, Consume, Die, because that is exactly what our corrupt government needs us to do.

Why?

I control me and I can tell you it is no easy job being rebellious, it takes courage, discipline and effort to be totally in control of one's mind and NOT be influenced by all the lies that our corrupt government throws our way.

I would NOT be successful if I had listened to the government, and I sure would NOT be a millionaire. I would NOT have this amazing life I have created and most of all I would NOT be happy.

This once-great country has gone to shit. Can't say this, can't say that because some brain-dead idiot might be offended. No one wants to take responsibility, living the 'blame game' life. How would your life be if, like me, you did not care what you said, what anyone thought of you, your actions and your results? Your life, like mine, would be amazing!

Is that the life you would like? Or are you going to continue to be controlled, be the sheep NOT the shepherd? Remember, people without ambition end up working for people with ambition.

The most successful people on earth do things differently, they are brave and rebellious, they get results. To be successful in every aspect of your life you need CONFIDENCE. It is that very quality that has carried me through life, making me the amazing person I am today.

Are you ready? The journey is going to be hard; you will suffer knockbacks, it will not be easy.

You WILL HAVE TO WORK HARD. Are you prepared? Are you prepared to do that? ARE YOU?

Read on!

Introduction

A very quiet boy always felt he was being left out. Last to be picked at football, sitting alone at the school disco, being excluded from activities every other child was enjoying. That boy left school and found the big wide world was no different, even more cruel in fact, but on a grander scale. This boy, now a man, realised that if you want life to be fair, you and only you can change the problems in your life which are getting you down.

This man had to change. No one was going to give him what he needed most, CONFIDENCE. He had to develop it himself.

Tired of being excluded, he took the first of many positive steps in his life and started to learn Kung-Fu.

To date, that man is an:

Eighth Dan Shaolin Kung-Fu Grandmaster.

A Kung-Fu Expert.

A Television and Film Stuntman who has amassed over 700 television and film credits.

A Stunt Co-ordinator.

A Guinness World Record Holder for his fantastic achievements in his stunt work.

An Author.

An International Speaker.

A Strategist.

A Millionaire.

Introduction

And THE MOST CONFIDENT MAN IN THE WORLD TODAY.

That man is me, Riky Ash.

If I am capable of developing and cultivating such confidence into my life, so can you.

Only YOU can change your life to become more confident.

You have a much greater advantage than I ever had. Someone to help you. Someone who has been there and proved that you can take yourself from loser to chooser.

Whether you are looking at this book in a library, a book shop or have borrowed it from a friend, do read it; this book has positive help and information for you to develop a confident and more rewarding life.

I MUST WARN YOU! I am direct, I tell it how it is, I DO NOT DO Political Correctness.

I am OUTSPOKEN and very proud of that quality.

I have authority.

I am strong and powerful and most of all I am unique.

Enjoy your reading, as you will discover after each time you read my book, you and others will notice within yourself a more happy, positive, and confident person beginning to develop.

A confidence that will remain with you throughout your whole life and reward you with great success and complete happiness.

Your author,
Riky Ash

Words of Wisdom

After having successfully overcome more than my fair share of problems in life I began to realise that it did not matter what my problem was, the most important factor was my state of mind.

Quite simply, if you faced up to your problem, no matter how bad your situation was at that present time or how you were then feeling, as long as you had the confidence to believe in yourself in time, your situation did improve for the better.

I never liked going to school, I hated school, it was not the learning that I disliked but the people I had to learn with. Because I was never a team player or one of the lads I was ostracised, and so found that throughout my life I will always be more of an individual rather than one of the crowd. When I look back now, I am pleased I was never a team player or one of the lads, because I did better than anyone at my school. I became the most successful pupil ever to attend Top Valley Comprehensive School, Nottingham, and not being a so-called team player made me the person I am today, unique.

I was born to shine.

To get me through the most unpleasant days of my life I developed a way to help me survive and I still adopt this method today. Why? Because it works. Whatever is happening now in my life that I am not happy with I use a positive attitude in my mind and say:

IT IS ONLY TEMPORARY.

It works. It works for me, and it will work for you. Remember, maintain that positive mental attitude and whatever gets in your way will only ever be temporary.

Life for me at times was shite. Did I allow the negativity to affect me? NO, what I did was use the emotive state to realise something had to change, I had to change to make my life better. Was I prepared to change? YES!

I was prepared to work and prepared to WORK HARD. To make my life the best it could possibly be, did I succeed? I sure did.

Enjoy reading my book and learning about the many ways you too can make your life the best it can possibly be.

You too will have to be prepared to WORK HARD. Just like I did.

Use your confidence in a positive and rewarding way to help yourself and others become better people.

I wish you the best of health and every happiness life can bring.

RIKY ASH

CHAPTER 1

MY STORY OF SUCCESS

What is confidence and why is it so important in our lives? Think about those experiences when you would have liked to have more confidence to carry out a task, say something in a conversation or try something completely new and just needed that extra push to carry you forward.

Many times in my teenage years I missed out on opportunities because I lacked the confidence in myself to do the things I really wanted to do. Only after taking up Kung-Fu – and believe me I put this off for many years because I lacked the confidence to pick up the telephone and enquire about lessons – did my life start to change for the better. Through regular Kung-Fu training I became healthier, happier and developed a positive outlook upon my life.

People who knew me as a very shy quiet person began to notice a much more confident and powerful person starting to develop. A person who noticed that the more confident I was, the more envied and hated I became. Did this affect me? NO, it was just what I expected. With my confidence, self-belief and positive state of mind I created a saying that I still use to this very day and you can use it too: FUEL FOR MY FIRE.

As my life progressed in a positive direction and I became successful, I found a negative attitude towards me by some of my friends. As a very astute individual I was able to establish that they had that awful disease by the name of JEALOUSY. The more successful I became the more their jealousy eroded them. What I was able to establish was that they were insecure and inadequate, and no matter what they said or thought of me they were not going to affect or control my life and my future. They were simply, The Shit on My Shoes.

I became bulletproof, nothing affected me. Never believe that one can be overconfident. It is simply not possible. It is the kind of shite psychologists peddle to try to warrant their worth. The more jealous and negative a person was towards me, was more FUEL FOR MY FIRE. It was an amazing motivator to drive me forward to become even more powerful and successful. Say I cannot run a mile, and I would run two miles. Whatever they said, I did more and yes, it pissed them off. It pissed them off so much they are still stinking of piss to this very day, and I love it.

I knew from a very young age that I was different. I never had any fear, and nothing frightened me. I was unique. I was BORN TO SHINE. The style of martial art I practise is called Shaolin Kung-Fu. To date (2024) I hold the rank of Eighth Dan Grandmaster. I am one of the highest exponents of Shaolin Kung-Fu in the world today. Just to put that into perspective, think footballers or racing drivers who are at the very top of their game. That is where I am, one of the world's best.

That twenty-year-old boy who was frightened to pick up the telephone to enquire about lessons is now one of the highest exponents of Kung-Fu in the world.

I am a television and film Stuntman, a Stunt Co-ordinator, an actor, an author and an international speaker known as "The Strategist".

Let's not forget a cabinet maker and a skilled craftsman. I would never have had the life I have today if I did not have CONFIDENCE and SELF-BELIEF. So let's look at where it all began. My journey to becoming the most confident and fearless man in the world today.

The major turning point for me was in 1987 when I was just 19 years old. Why was it that so many people were having so much fun and having the time of their lives in a time when cash was king? Why was my life stagnant? I was working at Thomas Pearson, a fine furniture maker and restorer in Netherfield, Nottingham, as a cabinet maker, earning at the time £75 per week, which is the equivalent of £261 today (2024).

I enjoyed every second of being a cabinet maker. This was a major turning point in my life going from boy to man, experiencing the tough life of the world of work, not the false picture that the Thatcher Government was painting. The working and social environment was sexist, racist, homophobic and not politically correct.

I worked with real people who taught me what real life was all about, it was survival taken to a whole new level. We did what we needed to do to survive, every day was a comedy, the best six years a teenage boy becoming a man could experience. I was surrounded by negative people, the tradesmen I worked with were all doom and gloom and the more they spoke in a negative way the more negative events happened to them.
My work colleagues and friends laughed at me when I said I was going to be rich, famous and super successful. They constantly put me down, which created my 'nothing ruffles my feathers' attitude and an even greater drive to be successful. Today people are not physically or mentally tough, crying every moment that someone calls them a name, claiming, "I've been offended, that's offensive, apologise." Pathetic, and the media is no better, peddling such shit instead of educating people to become mentally strong. I was brought up on the very strong saying, 'sticks and stones may break my bones but names will never hurt me.'

You simply cannot offend me, it is not possible, as I do not find any words you may throw my way as offensive, say what you like, your words will have no effect whatsoever, I am mentally and physically tough. There are far too many mardy bastards in the world today claiming they have been offended; what they need is to grow a pair of balls and a big pair at that.

Until I had passed my driving test and could afford a car, I walked two miles every morning to get a lift from miserable Nev, who was a wood veneerer, a dull individual who lived a negative life. At the end of a hard day miserable Nev would drop me off and I would walk the two miles home.

Hard work was instilled into me by my mum, Catherine, who was brought up in Southern Ireland with the very strict upbringing that if you want anything in life you have to work hard for it. I never believed in borrowing money, I never received pocket money, and every penny mattered to me. To date I have never had a loan or mortgage, and I never will.

I bought a £300 Ford Escort van; it was the best I could afford, no insurance and only the tax and MOT that came with it. As I said, the 1980s was survival, you did what you needed to do to survive and if that meant not giving our thieving government any more money than they deserved that is exactly what you did. In my mind they deserve nothing for the appalling, irresponsible way they run this country.

In 1987 to earn extra money I did what was referred to as 'jobs on the side'. I managed to secure some work doing painting and decorating and in the hot summer of 1987 I secured a contract to redecorate a flat that a landlord was going to rent out in the Mapperley area of Nottingham.

I was up on a stepladder, wallpapering, and out of the window opposite me I saw that outside a company by the name of Cavendish Finance was parked a red Ferrari. On the opposite side of the road a new UPVC window company had opened and parked outside there was a white Porsche 911 Cabriolet. Now most people in Nottingham had never seen these types of cars and the reaction when seeing them was again met with negativity and jealousy. My reaction was always the opposite: I admired people who had worked hard and rightly rewarded themselves. I have always loved Lamborghinis and that day motivated me so much.

I wanted that life; there was I in my £300 van and there were people driving cars worth tens of thousands of pounds, I wanted some. I was astute enough to know that as a cabinet maker I was never going to afford a Lamborghini and afford the amazing life I had set myself. I was also astute enough to understand that the government did not want me to be successful and was my ultimate enemy. Governments are powerless unless you are subservient, and I sure was not going to be anyone's bitch.

I left Thomas Pearson in 1990 to set up my own cabinet making and joinery business. In a time when we were suffering another recession, regardless of this, the positive was that at the age of 22 I had now escaped 'the rat race'. When woodworking was quiet I would do gardening work and anything that could make me money. I understood the quality of being resourceful, I was a hard worker and no matter what was happening in the world it was not going to hold back my journey to great confidence and success.

With Confidence

I was also a Kung-Fu instructor. My style of Kung-Fu is the originator of all martial arts; every martial art today has its ancestry in Shaolin Kung-Fu. Shaolin Kung-Fu was developed by a monk by the name of Bodhidharma who also created Zen Buddhism. It is the study of animals, how they fight, survive and defend themselves.

Now human beings are by far the most pathetic animal which has ever walked this earth, the reason being, does an eagle say, "I am not going to soar to the greatest heights, in case I upset another bird?" Does a cheetah say, "I am not going to run the fastest to catch my prey in case other cheetahs laugh at me?" No, they do not, and nor should you.

Are you going to walk this earth concerning yourself with what other people think? No, you are not! After reading, absorbing and adapting my words into your life, you are never going to be bothered by what another person says or thinks of you, whether it is positive or negative. They are INSIGNIFICANT.

Well, did I listen to their desperation? I listened, as I always do. I will always listen to both sides of a debate or argument and then decide. What I will never do is allow people who are the shit on my shoes to persuade me otherwise.

If our corrupt Government tells me to walk through door A then I am going through door B. Whatever they say I am doing the opposite because I know the shite they try to peddle to the people is for their benefit only and NOT MINE. I would never have the life I have today if I did not have the social intelligence to think this way. Everything I have done has paid off; did it pay off for my friends in the 1980s and my work colleagues who were racked in debt with ugly lives and ugly wives, because they lacked the confidence to live their life their way?

Work hard, and you too will have unrivalled confidence not to be conned by another person's negative influence. Remember, you MUST WORK HARD. Confidence is a developed state of mind. You cannot fake confidence, you can fake being rich, you can fake success; however, You cannot FAKE BEING CONFIDENT.

Do Not And Never Be Put Off An Idea Or Vision Of Something You Wish To Pursue Because Of Someone Else's Opinion.

Remember it is your life, and you and only you should make the final decision. By doing this you cannot blame anyone but yourself if things do not quite turn out how you would have liked them to. I have made many mistakes throughout my life, and until the last nail is driven into my coffin, I will still make them. What makes me unique from many individuals is that I have the personality to first acknowledge I have made a mistake, secondly admit I have made a mistake, and thirdly learn from that mistake. I do not and never have used 'the blame game', blaming others, blaming life, I endure. If things do not turn out as you expected them to and you did not apply yourself with dedication, discipline, hard work and effort you only have yourself to blame.

Sadly, we live in a world today where everyone wants to blame everyone else for their failings. DO NOT BE THAT PERSON! YOU MUST TAKE RESPONSIBILITY!

Face Up To Your Own Decisions

You made the decision, live by it. Do not blame others for your mistakes. Also remember to learn from your mistakes. Life has taught me some very valuable lessons which have formed me. Believe me when I say it has not always been an easy life. The good times and the very bad times have made me the person I am today. I am still using past experiences both positive and negative to help me move forward, and better myself to work hard for the best life I can possibly create.

I have developed a reputation for being outspoken. Some would say this is a fault in me or a bad habit; I see it totally differently. I see my outspokenness as an asset which gives me the ability, confidence and most of all, courage, to speak my mind. This is an attitude one will benefit from. As you progress through my book it will become noticeable through my own experiences that there is no secret to becoming more confident. The tools are all around you throughout your life. Pick them up, practise with them and you will, through time and patience, become better and more confident in your life.

Believe In Yourself

If you do not believe in yourself, how can you expect anyone else to believe in you?

When I decided I wanted to be a Stuntman many of my friends laughed at me, and very few thought I would ever make it. Some so-called friends even tried to put me off by attempting to fill my mind with negative thoughts. For every person that said I would not succeed, it gave me so much more drive and energy to achieve my goal and prove them wrong. My dream of becoming a Stuntman was very difficult, however realistic. I was physically fit, enthusiastic and most of all through my Kung-Fu training, dedicated and confident enough to believe in myself and I was prepared for hard work.

You only have to look at my stunt website to see how much I have achieved. You too will achieve as much or as little as you would like, but remember it is down to you and only you to make it happen. If you are a lazy person you will fail, no matter what you do you will fail. If you are not prepared for hard work, forget reading any further; if you are the type of person who expects everything to fall from the sky and this perfect life form around you, you have already failed, life just does not happen that way.

You Have To Make It Happen

As you read this part of my book you may or may not have the ability and licence to drive a car. When we first think of taking driving lessons, we also think of more than just driving a car, we think of the freedom this will give us, employment opportunities and many other great reasons to learn.

Now do the skills needed to drive a car come to you with the licence, without any input from yourself? You know the answer to this already, nothing worth having in life comes easy, we all have to work hard to get what we would like and need. It is the same with learning to drive, you have to first want to learn, then be dedicated, to put the time and effort into taking lessons, learning the theory and then taking the driving test. Then be determined if you at first fail the test to put more practice in to eventually achieve your goal.

After you pass your driving test that is not the end of it, you are still learning and for those out there who claim to be a good driver, until you can drive like a Stuntman you know nothing about driving, I can tell you that.

Be Patient

Nothing worth having in life comes to us easily. This has been said many times in life for a reason because it is true. If you want it you have to go out and get it. If you want it to happen you have to make it happen. If you want it to work you have to make it work. Be patient and work hard towards your goal. Channel your energy positively and eventually you will achieve. If you have unrealistic expectations and expect everything to fall at your feet and skills develop overnight, WAKE UP; it just does not happen like that.

Do you think my amazing confidence and great success dropped from the sky and landed around me? No, I have worked so hard for everything I have achieved, and I am an advocate of HARD WORK and still work on my confidence and personal development every waking hour. Even in my dreams, I am the bollox!

A very interesting study is that of animal behaviour. When they hunt for food, some animals rely on their ability to sit still for hours to catch their prey. They know that without patience they do not make a kill and ultimately do not eat. Being impatient also leads us as human beings to frustration which can ultimately cause stress. So remember next time you are sitting in heavy traffic you have two options. You can accept the situation you are in and be patient, as you know it will eventually clear, or you can simply get out of your car, leave it where it is and walk away. This is not the best option. Accepting the situation you are in eliminates stress instantly.
I always have a volume of reading matter in whatever vehicle I choose to take that day. There have been many times where I have been held up in

traffic and sat for many hours with the engine turned off. I can utilise this time by reading. I know in time the situation will improve, there is nothing I can do to change it, however I can adapt to the situation to suit me, and that is exactly what I do. I also have a very advanced telephone system built into my vehicle, today known as infotainment. With my engine switched off I can utilise the opportunity to make telephone calls; this passes the time, I do not get frustrated and when the traffic is in motion I have achieved, where around me most people are bored and remember, ONLY BORING PEOPLE GET BORED.

Remember Not Everyone Is Like You

How many times have you arranged to meet with someone or have planned to do something with a friend and on the day they either turn up late and ruin the whole day's plans or simply phone and cancel right at the last moment without any consideration for your hard work and planning? This infuriates you, makes you angry. Why? Because you would not have done that to anyone.

Now this is where the truth kicks in. NOT EVERYONE IS LIKE YOU. Personally I am a very reliable person and will not let people down. If I say I am going to do something I do it; this is well known of me. I am a doer not a sayer. With the erratic nature of my work as a Stuntman there are times when I do have to cancel things as work does take priority, and because of this I always keep people informed, so at least they know where they stand. Having the social intelligence to do the simplest of things and keep people informed, is so easy to do; however certain individuals seem to find the basics of life fail them.

Most people only think of one person, themselves. They are not bothered by who they upset when they arrive late, or do not even bother to turn up at all. Obviously when it affects you it becomes your problem, or you make it your problem and you get angry and let it bother you. Your anger and disappointment does not bother the person who let you down one bit, they probably let several people down that day and will continue doing this until people like yourself either drop them as friends or accept THAT NOT EVERYONE IS LIKE YOU.

The truth is most people are LAZY, UNRELIABLE AND THOUGHTLESS and will always stay that way. Coping with this is simple, DO NOT LET IT BOTHER YOU. Look at who you are and what you have achieved, and you will see what I mean.

People who are selfish and unreliable introduce stress into their lives, they constantly moan about things not working out for them and look at your life as the life that they would most want. The reason their life is such a mess is through their own selfish attitude, being unreliable, always turning up late, constantly letting people down. They simply try and cram far too much into one day, it does not work out for them, and they just do not know why. They have chaotic lifestyles, they say, "I forgot, I lost it, I can't find it, it's broken, I have the phone but not the charger." The thing that needs charging most is their useless brain.

They Have No Management In Their Life

So for you to become a stronger and more confident person you are never going to let these kinds of people bother you again. If you arrange something with a friend and they have good reason to cancel or be late, fair enough; if this becomes a regular occurrence then think how much you really want to put into planning a day with a person like this who is more than likely going to let you down anyway. I call them loose cannons.

Who needs friends like that anyway. You will never be able to change a person to make them more reliable and thoughtful towards others, they have to do this themselves and eventually a person's unreliable attitude always catches up with them. Leave them to it, do not make it your problem. When you have arranged something good and they do not get the invite, because of their unreliable nature, they will eventually get the message. I have done that many times with my unreliable friends, I stopped involving them and that was the end of them. I am ruthless; if you do not meet my high standards I will drop you.

So you have now learned a very simple lesson, DO NOT LET IT BOTHER YOU. You are becoming more confident already. Do not worry about losing friends; in life, like most things, friends simply come and go. The good ones will stay around for life, but look back at your circle of friends, it is ever-changing. I do not see my school friends anymore and my first circle of friends has long gone. Through my Kung-Fu training friends have come and gone and the same can be said of the friends I have made through being a Stuntman. People change, situations change. Friends will simply come and go and that is life. Accept it.

I have removed so many unreliable people from my life, I only have positive, productive, reliable people around me. I am very strict: if you do not meet my expected standards you are gone, I do not suffer fools. I do not waste my time on the nobodies of life going nowhere fast.

When you restructure your life, create your near-perfect environment, as your confidence develops more strongly you will be able to drop the losers in life just like you would drop a stone into a pond. You do have to be ruthless; however, that ruthlessness has not been created by you, it has been created by those individuals whose unreliable nature was affecting you, so remove them, move on and forget it.

So why do we need confidence anyway?

Would you like to be successful?

Let's briefly focus on success. You are unwell and need surgery, would you like that surgery to be successful? With a positive outcome?

You need a confident skilful surgeon, one who has self-belief, has worked and trained hard to be the best that they can possibly be, you need a Hawkeye Pierce out of M*A*S*H.

I do not want, a 'I think I am good enough', or a 'I think I can do it' or a 'I hope I can do it'.

I want a 'I CAN DO IT BECAUSE I AM THE BEST. That is the kind of surgeon I want, a confident one. Same when I board a plane, I want the captain to be confident, to be able to get the plane's ass off the runway, into the air, fly it and land it safely.

No Place For Modesty

Would you like that kind of confidence? Well, if you adopt the correct mindset and work hard, and I mean work hard, you are going to have to work hard on yourself to achieve. Never concern yourself with what anyone thinks of you, good or bad.

Confidence is a STATE OF MIND.

Having the confidence to speak your mind no matter how controversial.

Never being influenced by another person's thoughts or opinions.

Creating your own path in life.

Never allowing the government to control you.

Having the power to control yourself.

Developing the courage to be unique.

Standing up for your beliefs and not being brainwashed.

I want you to establish this to put what you have read so far into perspective.

If I did not have confidence I would not have:

My beautiful home in the countryside bought outright with cash.

I would never have progressed with my Kung-Fu, becoming an Eighth Dan Grand Master and I will progress to Tenth Dan Doctor of Kung-Fu.

I would not have my amazing Lamborghini.

I would never have become a Stuntman, Stunt Co-ordinator and actor.

I would never have become an international speaker or author.

I would never have become wealthy.

The success of my life is attributed to my unrivalled confidence.

And do you know if I had been weak enough to listen to those negative people who said I could never do it, where would my life be today?

I am simply the best! And here is the best bit, YOUR LIFE CAN BE LIKE THAT TOO.

That is what confidence does, there are no negatives.

POINTERS TO HELP YOU

- DO NOT ALLOW SOMEONE ELSE TO CONTROL YOUR FUTURE.
- BE PREPARED TO ACCEPT RESPONSIBILITY FOR YOUR ACTIONS.
- IF YOU DO NOT BELIEVE IN YOURSELF NO ONE ELSE WILL.
- GO OUT THERE AND MAKE IT HAPPEN.
- BE PREPARED TO WORK HARD.
- BETTER THINGS WILL DEVELOP IN TIME.
- DO NOT ALLOW THE ACTIONS OF OTHERS TO BECOME YOUR PROBLEM.

Remember This Is Your Life

Confidence, just like a 35mm photograph, takes time to develop.
Read on and in time you will have the best, most rewarding life one can ever achieve.

PROVIDING YOU ARE PREPARED!

CHAPTER 2

CONTROLLING THE UNCONTROLLABLE

A decision that someone else has made, that adversely affects your life and creates an emotional upheaval does not have to destroy you. Do not fall to pieces, use the experience to become a much stronger and better person and learn from it. Emotional problems which bring on stress and worry can rapidly wear the most confident of individuals down. A degree of time is needed for the individual to get themselves back to rational thinking.

Firstly, whether it may be a relationship break-up, loss of job, or another issue that is beyond your control, do not blame yourself, unless however it was your fault. Only look back at the experience to take positive lessons away, to use in future situations. You must keep yourself busy, occupying your time with positive activities to remove your thoughts away from the shock experience. YOU ARE NOW CONTROLLING THE UNCONTROLLABLE. Look to your future in a positive manner. If it was a relationship break-up convince yourself your next companion will be far better, and believe me, they always are.

When a long-term girlfriend ended our four-year relationship on the grounds of wanting to lead a single girl's life, I was devastated. The shock was something else. My health and career as a Stuntman was excellent. Life was just great, and then suddenly without warning she ended our relationship, a situation totally out of my control.

Being a confident person I was able to turn a negative situation into a positive one by looking at all of her good and bad points, where the bad points strongly outweighed the good ones. It was this analysis that helped me realise just how selfish a person she was, and this gave me the drive to pick myself up, dust myself down and move on. I am much wiser and more astute now to know exactly what I want from a relationship, and today I would have never tolerated her spoilt brat behaviour.

One important fact in a relationship break-up is to accept that the relationship is over and move on. From this bad experience I then looked at the positives and now know that I will never tolerate a selfish girlfriend again. A lesson learned. Looking at my life now I am engaged to a fantastic lady. I would never have had a happy fulfilling relationship with 'Bitch Features'. She was an inadequate girlfriend and always would be. A liability to anyone who had the misfortune to involve themselves with her.

In any emotional upheaval you must be *in control* of your thoughts to generate them positively. This will help you climb back up that ladder to even greater happiness where you can look to your future with ambition and enthusiasm. This is a new start. Be excited and confident as better things will definitely come your way, as they did for me. When negative experiences affect my life, they only affect me in a positive way. I learn so much from these life events as they make me train harder, become richer, and even more successful.

When problems arise, we can become very dependent on other people, but when other people are the creation of the problem in the first place it then becomes a completely different situation. Take, for instance, relationship breakdowns. When one person decides they no longer want to be with the other person, if you are the one who is being rejected it feels like your whole world has just fallen apart. You may have experienced many relationships coming to an end, and one would think that this experience would make you become immune to emotional upset. It is actually completely the opposite. When a relationship comes to an end through no fault of your own, regardless of your level of confidence, you are going to feel hurt, but remember a very important point:

IT IS ONLY TEMPORARY

The way you are feeling when your relationship ends is not necessarily how you will be feeling in six weeks' time or even six months' time. We all experience a state of emotional upheaval. We find it hard to eat, sleep, concentrate and even enjoy the things that make us happy. When the hatred and anger have worn off, we have to start to pick ourselves up and carry on. Being a more confident person does not and will not make you immune to emotional upset, however being confident will give you the advantage to realise the break-up was no big thing, and in life these things happen. As you are now aware, as time goes by you start to feel better in yourself, you start to get out more, meet new people and find your life is becoming more rewarding, OR ARE YOU?

As a confident person you will always see the light at the end of the tunnel, glass half full, any problem or negative experience will never control you, as you will be in control by your positive attitude.

ACCEPT REALITY

Do not get upset by things you cannot change. If you had planned a day out, and your day relied on good weather, and on that day the weather turned out to be dreadful, do not get worked up about something that is completely out of your control. Things change. It has never consistently rained since you were born, has it?

The reality is that you cannot change life. However, you can change your mind, and how you react to it. I hated every second of comprehensive school. I hated the people I had to sit in class with. I hated the education system. If I knew then what I know now I would have left home and joined the circus, or got a job with Mr Kipling, filling tarts with cream.

For me school was a cesspit of negativity. Nottingham was a very negative city, however even as young as 14 I knew I would be successful as I did not act and think like other children. My reality was that I had to attend school and tolerate 'The Shit On My Shoes' while I was there; however, I did not have to live with such evil. I was determined to progress, whereas other children were not.

My coping strategy consisted of a chart on my bedroom wall with every day that year I had to attend school. Once I returned home at the end of the day, I would cross off the day, the week, the month; my leaving day of the 27 May 1983 was my inspiration, can you remember the day you left school? I never went back to collect my exam results: they are still sitting on the school reception to this day. They can stay there, as even back in 1983 I was determined to be successful without a piece of paper saying otherwise.

BEING RESILIENT

If it happens it happens, cope with it, accept it. Have the courage to PICK YOURSELF UP, DUST YOURSELF DOWN AND CARRY ON. Life will improve, do not allow yourself to be controlled by another person's decision, you take control, not them, they are insignificant now, THEY DO NOT MATTER. This also applies to our corrupt government, have the bollox to stand up to them. They do not care about you; they never have, and they never will. YOU need to care about YOU.

It is very important to remember and realise that things will not always go your way. Some people get very irritated when they do not get their own way and act like a young child throwing a tantrum. You must accept that sometimes you will lose the game, or you may not get the job you so longed for, or the shelf just fell down because you trusted someone else to do the job you would have done much better. So when things do not go your way this is where you can control what is going on around you.

Firstly:

DO NOT LET THE SIMPLE THINGS GET TO YOU. What is happening to you right now is only temporary. You have read this before in my book and you will keep reading it again and again and again, because it is true. You are riding the rollercoaster of life; this is how it is and this is how it always will be. You will experience setbacks throughout your life and the more ambitious you are the more susceptible to setbacks you will be.

Life at times can be a barrel of shite.

Many times I have planned to do something I consider to be very important and, through no fault of my own, I am let down by others. Well, now it has no effect on me whatsoever, as I do now tend to expect people to be unreliable and let me down. So with this mindset, I am never surprised or angry when it happens. I only surround myself with positive successful people, I am ruthless, as you now know, I do not take prisoners, if you do not meet my very high standards I will remove you from my life, and I do not allow people to leech off me. I am very selective.

Concentrate on yourself, remember to always take regular exercise. This in itself will make you feel so much better; as we know, exercise makes us feel good after our training session has been completed. YOU MUST BE DEDICATED. If you are not willing to put in the effort that life requires you will not become the best person you possibly can be, you will not become confident, positive and ultimately successful.

You have to WORK HARD. You have to be prepared to work hard on YOU!

As a practitioner of regular exercise, I do have to admit that some aspects of training are not that pleasant. A hard workout can be very uncomfortable; however, the feeling I get when it is complete is amazing and also do remember the importance of a good diet.

I have trained both my body and mind regularly since I was 17.

I am not going to lecture you on what you should or should not eat; you should know for yourself what is good for you and what you should avoid, however that is your choice. This book is not intended to be about diet and nutrition, so you should look at what you eat and drink, and decide if you are doing the right thing.

Sleep is vital, without it we will die and very quickly indeed. With the lack of it we will not operate efficiently, we will make mistakes which can lead to accidents and fatalities.

You can read all sorts of research into how much sleep we should get; however, you tend to know yourself what works for you. I do not buy into what scientists say, they all seem to have a differing opinion, there were no scientists around in prehistoric times and we have managed to still be walking the earth today. I created MY OWN RULES FOR LIFE. I am not influenced by others, I assess and make my own mind up about my life and what I believe, and believe me, I do not believe scientists.

You know yourself, you know your own body, so you work out just how much sleep you require. Remember, the lack of sleep will catch up on you, and sooner or later, if you are not getting enough, you will burn yourself out. So do not neglect the important things in your life as good health leads to happiness and we all aspire to be happy. When things do not quite go to plan, next time just think of how you will now control the situation to work to your advantage. When you look at a situation, look at it with a more positive attitude and inevitably things will always be more favourable and work to your advantage.

I can only explain to you through my own experiences. I realised at a young age that if you truly want something you have to MAKE IT HAPPEN and if things do not quite go to plan there will always be a way to change them for the better. You have to first want to change things and then have the courage to change them. People are so frightened of change: change happens and will always happen.

In 2006, ironically the very year this book was first published, I bought a house on the edge of countryside. I moved from my first ever house which was a two-bedroom semi-detached that I bought outright with cash in 2000 because I was a very astute guy. I then purchased a house that needed modernisation. I was more than capable of taking this on and between my stunt work over the course of two years I converted it into a comfortable marketable home, which I sold on in 2006 for three times what I paid for it. This allowed me to move to a four-bedroom executive home which I bought for £250,000 cash, yes cash, no mortgage as I do not believe in borrowing money.

The first seven years of living there were good. I knew it was not my dream home and, in many ways, not the right home for me; however, it did increase in value, which is always a bonus. There were farmer's fields opposite me which were outlined for development. In 2013 everything changed: permission for, are you ready, 3000 houses and shit houses at that was granted. Four different developers building shite homes at nearly 24 hours a day, houses for the 'Shit4Brainz' in life, the clueless and totally fucking clueless at that.

My beautiful view I looked forward to coming home to was ruined in a matter of weeks. I had objected to the build; however, we all know just how corrupt local authorities are, so there was no chance that petitions and objection letters were going to have any impact. I was one of the very few neighbours who had the bollox to actually fight the build. I was finding it was grinding me down and not the kind of grinding I was used to, so I needed to take positive action. I could not stop the build, however believe me, the developers hated me because I managed to delay it at their cost.

Time to turn a negative experience into a positive one and that is exactly what I did and leave the 'Shit4Brainz' in life to enjoy living in Shitsville.

The developers did me a very big favour as, unknowingly, they placed their sales office directly opposite my home. I saw an opportunity. I do not do estate agents; when I sold my first house I controlled everything, made a For Sale sign, conducted my own conveyancing, did not engage the services of a solicitor and saved myself around £4000 Now that's confidence!

I did exactly the same in my current situation. This time I had the advantage of a ready-made supply of buyers, firstly coming to view Shitsville. They could not avoid seeing my For Sale sign and to grab their attention even more, on busy weekends I would take my Lamborghini out of its garage and park the fucker right in front of their eyes. It did not take long before I had secured my buyer. Deal done, I was off. I put everything into storage and lodged with a friend; this was no inconvenience as I spend a considerable time of my year in hotels nationally and internationally.

In 2018 I found what can only be described as my dream home, a thousand times better than the home I had owned previously, bought again outright with £315,000 in cash. Successful! My personality is one of confidence, courage, determination and self-belief. Regardless of how

I was educated at school I rejected conventional education and crafted what works for me.

Being confident in all aspects of my life makes my life easy.

It is known that in disasters the people who adopt a positive attitude and show confidence are the ones who survive, because they only see the situation as temporary and through their positive attitude instantly behave in a constructive manner. Those people who just give up right from the start do not survive for very long, they end up being tonight's dinner. This is a true example of controlling the uncontrollable, as now you are in the situation, do something about it to survive.

I did exactly this with my home. I was disruptive towards the build, however I was not going to stop it, what eventually happened was that Shitsville did me a very big favour, it forced me to take action and that action created an opportunity to better my home life, move and have my dream home. I do believe that if Shitsville had never been built I would still be living there now.

As none of us really know what our future holds, being a confident person will always give you that added advantage as when problems do arise, and they will, that is life, you will be in a better frame of mind if you adopt the ITS ONLY TEMPORARY attitude and then start to CONTROL THE UNCONTROLLABLE. It is as simple as that and it really is simple.

It has been mentioned many times before, and it will be mentioned constantly throughout my book. Those thoughts good or bad are placed into your mind by you and you only, so delete all negative thoughts and only concentrate on what really matters, the positive ones, as it is these thoughts that will make you a stronger and more successful person and ultimately a happier one at that.

You are now some way further to controlling the uncontrollable.

As I alluded to earlier and will continue to refer throughout my book, it is the thoughts that enter and leave your mind that are put there by one person and one person only, YOU. So if you put negative thoughts into your mind what can you expect back from yourself? From now on start to train your thought process and be a more positive person and just see how things start to work better for you. It is not difficult as you are the one in control.

It will take hard work and dedication. Some years ago, I dated 'Miss Negative'. To her, life was shite. The real truth was that it was her that was shite, not life; she was a Ferrari without an engine, just tits & fanny and nothing else, one of life's losers. No matter what I said, what I did to help her she was not willing to help herself, she was lazy and would not work on her own self-development, she was draining. I established that she had to go, her negativity was bringing me down. A strong confident person like me needs to be surrounded by strong confident people, NOT Ferraris without engines. Have the confidence to remove the negativity out of your life and keep your association with negative people to a minimum.

YOU ARE NOW CONTROLLING THE UNCONTROLLABLE.

A final thought for you. I have been back to see what became of Shitsville and the visits just reinforced that I made the right move on the chess board of life. Houses and cars broken into. Gates and fences either broken or missing, a right shithole just as I predicted and I am never wrong.

I now live in paradise compared to where I was living. Life does have a way of creating an unexpected opportunity for us.

POINTERS TO HELP YOU

- OCCUPY YOUR MIND WITH POSITIVE ACTIVITIES.
- YOUR CURRENT PROBLEMS ARE ONLY TEMPORARY.
- ACCEPT REALITY.
- DO NOT ALLOW SIMPLE PROBLEMS TO GET YOU DOWN.
- BE RUTHLESS IN REMOVING ENERGY VAMPIRES FROM YOUR LIFE.

As you enter the next chapter, look back and remember that nothing, absolutely nothing, will ever get in your way again, because you are in control!

As one of my good friends, Roger, often says, "Fuck em!"

CHAPTER 3

A DISCIPLINED MIND

So how difficult or how easy is it to train your mind to constantly think positively? Some people find it very hard to think anything but negative thoughts and then wonder why they constantly experience problems and find it very difficult to cope with challenges when they arise.

What one needs is to develop a POSITIVE MENTAL ATTITUDE. Adopt this thought process and you will never be defeated. Constantly train your mind to only see the positive side to any situation and you will always endure.

Throughout our lives we will always experience problems, some very serious, some trivial, that is the nature of the beast. From a very early age we start to encounter difficulty, from playing as young children to progressing to school, the problems begin. An important fact most people tend to overlook is that all problems, regardless how great or minor, can be overcome. It is the way we attack our problem and the state of mind we adopt that decides how long or how short this matter will stay in our minds.

By the time you finish this chapter you will have developed a completely different mindset by using a technique I developed some years ago which works very well in all negative situations. It will work for you provided you have a disciplined mind.

IF IT IS GOING TO HAPPEN IT IS GOING TO HAPPEN

Many times we see a news story, and someone who witnessed a car crashing into a garden at speed says, "There could have been children playing in that garden and they would have been killed." The fact is, there were no children there, so no children were killed. Only concentrate on what has actually happened, not what could have happened. Remove any negative thoughts completely out of your mind.

Be very careful with the utter shite the government regularly peddle us. One of the biggest lies we endure on a near daily basis is the non-existent climate change, a term created entirely by governments and the media, and what is so sad is that most people actually believe this shit.

So let's just investigate this further. "So who told you that?" I ask people when they start spurting climate change shit. They don't know so I remind them, was it the media by any chance? Yes it was, through the many media outlets who our corrupt government control they are able to saturate every avenue available to them to brainwash you into believing such bollox.

How many times have you witnessed a news story that climate change does not exist? Never, because those scientists who have proved it does not will never get their findings broadcast or published in the mainstream media, that is exactly how governments work.

Climate change is nothing but propaganda.

Think back, if you will, to the Bogeyman; when we were very young children our parents would lie to us, claiming that if we played out the Bogeyman would capture us, and we would never be seen again. We believed it because we did not know any better, we were naive, impressionable and ignorant.

I ask you this question. Are you still naive, impressionable and ignorant? If you believe what the government says then you are, and not only that, you are vulnerable. What confidence does is destroy that vulnerability, it destroys naivety, it destroys ignorance, it makes you strong, it makes you powerful, it makes you independent.

To set the record straight, climate change does not and never has existed. What is currently happening to our planet is climate cycles and nothing else, everything in life goes around in a cycle. Our corrupt government needs you to be weak, they cannot control you unless you are subservient.

A Disciplined Mind

Are you really that weak a person that you will allow a nobody journalist or MP going nowhere fast to dictate your life? I sure am not.

I have the confidence to create my own set of rules for my life and climate change bollox does not even figure. We all know someone who is ALL DOOM AND GLOOM. They cannot and never will see the positive side in anything. They always have to look on the pessimistic side of life. It does not matter what they or others do it will fail: "It won't work – I am no good – They are no good" then to no one's surprise everything does go wrong.

If you bang a nail into a piece of wood and say in your mind, *I am going to hit my finger*, I always hit my finger, what happens? Yes, you smack your finger, thumb, the back of your hand and why, because your mind is very good at doing exactly what it is told. Its job is designed for that exact purpose, so start disciplining yourself and your mind and bring a positive and realistic attitude into your thinking. And when I say realistic, I do mean it, because regardless of how positive you can be, WE SIMPLY CANNOT FLY so do not go throwing yourself off the nearest tower block with the thought well Riky said, because you are right, Riky did say BE REALISTIC and you will be successful. Leave the jumping from tower blocks to me, that's my job. When you encounter a problem simply acknowledge its existence and concentrate your energy to finding a solution.

Some years ago, while working as a Stuntman, I met a person who was supplying props to a film I was working on. We became friends and I was able to establish that he had issues; all he was good at was being shit. Whatever he attempted to do he simply messed it up, blamed the tools he was using, blamed the weather, blamed others, blamed his upbringing but never himself.

No matter how much I tried to help him he did not take advice very well. So, let's look at me at the time. It was the year 2000. I had a very successful career as a Stuntman, having been able through hard work and astuteness to have bought my first house outright with cash. I was financially sound and a cool businessman. I was able to make anything out of anything, a craftsman, a Kung-Fu expert, so I had a pedigree.

I had proven myself as a very successful smart guy, who incidentally came from nothing and I mean absolutely nothing: I never received pocket money like most children did, my clothes hung off me as they were handed down to me by my brother, even today they would still be too big for me. My early life was harsh, my school and teenage years were miserable. However, I worked hard on myself to make my life better. So here I was helping and advising 'Fucked It Up' and he had the audacity to doubt me.

I dropped him like you would drop a stone into a pond.

The message here is a clear one: if someone is giving you advice to help improve your life and they have 'walked the walk' then they have every right to 'talk the talk'.

If you are going to take advice from anyone, be sure they know their shit first.

THE RIVER APPROACH

Life places enough obstructions in your way so do not place anymore obstructions yourself. Mentally absolutely anything can be overcome.

You approach a river, the answer to your problems lies on the opposite bank.
Do you:
A) – Turn back, walk away, turn your back on your problem? Your problem is still there.
B) – Look at ways of building a bridge or a tunnel, maybe find a boat and sail across. In other words have someone carry you across, building bridges and tunnels are only seen as ways of trying to buy yourself time.
C) – Get your feet wet, get completely wet and swim across using your own strength. This is your positive choice. You will not have been the first person to get completely wet, not the first person to ever have this problem. Remember you will not stay wet forever, you will eventually dry off.

PROBLEM SOLVED – PROBLEM RESOLVED

There is such an important lesson we can all learn from the river approach. Remember, you are not the first person ever to have encountered whatever problem you are experiencing. A friend once told me a very important fact when I was experiencing a difficult time in my life. His words were, "We have all been there." When I thought about what he had said he was right. We have and always will experience problems, we have to get on with life, keep ourselves busy and devote our energies to practical and creative activities that not only benefit ourselves, but also benefit others too and we will all start to feel a whole lot better.

So thank you for those words of advice, Roger, said to me back in 2004 when I was going through a relationship breakdown. Even with my personality I am still willing to take good advice on board, for we are forever learning.

Think about the things you really enjoy, the things that really make you happy, make you laugh. Even though you may be feeling down. Just for this moment think about someone, somewhere, something that truly makes you happy. Focus your mind right now, channel all your energy into those thoughts. Even if each day you give a little thought when feeling down to the happy times you will start to feel happy, and your motivation will become stronger to experience those happier times yet again.

It is very rare that I feel down; on those eventful days I go into my garage and just look at my Lamborghini. I love it, just looking at it gives me an instant lift. Opening it up and sliding inside, looking at the bull with the huge bollox on the steering wheel, then starting that V10 engine up, what a sound, what a feeling. Even watching Lamborghini videos on YouTube gives me an instant lift. When I was younger, I said in my teenage years that one day I would have a Lamborghini and I did, through determination and HARD WORK!

As I have said many times before and will keep saying it again and again, what you are experiencing when you are feeling down and depressed IS ONLY TEMPORARY; the negative thoughts in your mind are placed there by you. You are now going to start disciplining yourself to think and act in a much more positive manner and it will take discipline.

IF IT WORKED FOR ME IT WILL WORK FOR YOU

When I was growing up, I massively lacked confidence, was very shy and withdrawn and did not mix well with other children. I was excluded from so much of the games children played, and would watch from a distance as others played and wished I could play with them. When I entered comprehensive school, I still lacked the confidence most children my age seemed to have and it just became more and more difficult to fit in; there was I, missing out yet again. When I left school, nothing changed: I still lacked confidence and missed out on the enjoyment of being a teenager with a little cash to spend. When people meet me today, they do not believe I was the kind of person who lacked confidence and was shy and withdrawn.

Around the age of 19 I started to realise that I had to change, and I am sure glad I did, as I realised what I needed more than anything was the courage to be myself, and with this mindset I started to change. The process of becoming a more confident person did take time and the real turning point in my life, as you have previously read, was when I started to learn Kung-Fu. Through regular training any fighting art will make the quietest of individuals confident in time.

Do not kid yourself: confidence, just like anything in life worth having, will take time and in time I became confident enough to stand up for myself in an argument and ultimately developed the confidence to start dating girls. I quickly realised that most guys lacked confidence when it came to girls, so when I started to ask girls out and they were saying yes this was a real confidence boost. When they said no, I just moved on with the attitude, well it's your loss.

Through this strong mental attitude, I developed an immunity to rejection, and just carried on regardless. Now as an established Stuntman being confident is a necessary requirement to keep one safe. That is why I say, **IF IT WORKED FOR ME IT WILL WORK FOR YOU.** It will, believe me. A very quiet shy boy developed into a courageous Stuntman with a high degree of confidence which, remember, no one gave me. I developed it myself through a disciplined mind and self-belief. I knew I would succeed and for every knockback I experienced I learned a valuable lesson. As we continue on this rough journey through life, we will sometimes encounter knockbacks, and if we are to become successful in our own right, we must be mentally strong.

As many temptations are laid in our way, we start to realise that the road to misery can be a really smooth one. It is very easy to become weak in oneself and take drugs, abuse alcohol and lead a life of crime and unacceptable behaviour. If you desire to have a happy life, one with great health and reward, we have to work so hard to achieve this. When you take this option, you are travelling down a dirt track laden with potholes and you sometimes think, why am I on this hard road when all those around me seem to be having life so easy?

Yes, it is hard when you decide to dedicate your life to becoming the best person you possibly can. Remember in the long run that dirt track you are travelling along eventually arrives at a beautiful sandy beach with warm clear water. We do not need to explain the destination of the other road. We will let history speak for itself.

I will keep stressing that you MUST BE prepared to WORK HARD. Work hard on yourself, both physically and mentally.

HAVING THE CONFIDENCE TO BE YOURSELF

How many times have you wished you could just be yourself, be a more relaxed person around others and have your own opinion instead of always agreeing just to simply fit in? Well, you can if you truly want to.

When we look at the way most people dress, and the 'in' hairstyle they adopt, despite it looking completely ridiculous, and when people look back at the clothes and hairstyles they used to have, they themselves have to admit how daft they looked and all this is JUST TO FIT IN. Well, if that is fitting in I shall remain the unfashionable guy I am and have always been and JUST SIMPLY STAND OUT.

With Confidence

Today's society is making people weak, with a 'you can't say that' mentality as it might offend someone – bollox. One thing I was not going to do was allow political correctness to dictate my words, I have more about me than that. I would never have enjoyed great success if I were not the outspoken gentleman that I am today. I do not conform, never have, never will. I also hate diversity: it is ruining the country. The only consideration that one should be concerned with is MERIT. Can a person actually do the job? Nothing else should matter.

I cannot be offended, it is not possible to offend me, just think how rock solid your life would be if you had my personality. Not a day goes by when I don't view the news, and someone somewhere has been offended. I look at them and think, ***You pathetic piece of shit. Grow up, GROW SOME BALLS AND A FUCKIN BIG PAIR AT THAT AND STOP BEING A GIRL.***

Every day, someone out there is crying into their cornflakes because someone said some so-called hurtful words.

"I wish I had the confidence you have, Riky." Frequently, friends and acquaintances say those very words to me.

Confidence is attractive.

Confidence is powerful.

Confidence will get you positive results.

Confidence will bring you SUCCESS!

JUST BE YOURSELF

Why do you feel you have to follow the crowd to fit in? This is a total lack of confidence and a false belief that by looking and acting the same as others we will be accepted.

This is the usual mindset of people who feel they have to drink alcohol to fit into society and be accepted. Tests have been conducted on groups of people who on one evening were allowed to drink alcohol and on another evening were given non-alcoholic drinks without knowing: they felt exactly the same on both evenings. So in their minds they associate alcohol with having a good time. Well I do not drink alcohol at all and I can guarantee that a night out with me will be the best fun you will ever have and no alcohol needs to be consumed. However, if you do enjoy a drink then that is fair enough; DO remember that excessive drinking will seriously damage your body so make sure this pleasure does not lead to pain and always be sure your drinking does not have a negative effect on others. If it does, stop drinking and seek help right now.

As far as fashions are concerned, do not buy to fit in, buy because you like or you need.

From a very young age I was criticised by my own pathetic excuse of a father for not wanting to participate in playing sports. I hate sports and always have. They do not interest me. However, the good-for-nothing useless bastard forced me to play football and especially cricket; I hated both. If I refused to play he would beat me, and I do not mean a slap, I mean a beating, he would beat me with the metal tube of our vacuum cleaner. How dare I not want to play cricket? Instead of accepting that I was a unique individual and establishing what I did like, I was beaten and forced to play the sports that interested him.

I wanted an air pistol; he bought me a cricket bat and when I refused to play cricket he beat me with it. Today my father's appalling behaviour would warrant a healthy prison sentence. The positives I take from such a negative childhood is that it made me strong and determined that no one, absolutely no one, will ever control and dictate the direction my life will travel in.

It is very difficult to have the confidence to be individualistic. I have chosen to be an individual for many years now and do have the confidence to carry this off. There are more important things in life than to concern myself with what people think of me. I judge my success not by how many people like me, but by how many people actually dislike me. Because I know that most people dislike a very successful person, I know that the more people who dislike me, the more I am doing things right.

I have never wanted to fit in, I was born to stand out.

I ONLY HAVE TO JUSTIFY MY ACTIONS TO MYSELF

The problem with so many people is that they devote far too much time and energy to what people think of them. It is a simple fact that YOU CANNOT PLEASE EVERYONE. So please just one person: YOURSELF. It is so much easier that way. You may not have the confidence at this stage to think like this, but believe me, once you start to think like a confident person your mindset will be completely different. As I have said earlier, and I shall keep reminding you of this very important fact that will be the decider of you becoming confident:

ALL NEGATIVE THOUGHTS THAT ENTER YOUR MIND ARE ONLY PLACED THERE BY YOU.

You are now becoming aware of how your mind's thoughts affect your life.

SUPERSTITION

Why do some people have to rely on the thoughts related to superstitions? Surely in this day and age your mindset should have developed in a more constructive way, not to be guided by old wives' tales and rubbish that has entered your mind because someone said it was UNLUCKY. I do not believe in luck. Superstitions, just like religions, again are like PVC, manmade, they serve no positive function in life and if you are stupid enough to allow this to control you, sadly you are weak.

DO YOU WANT TO BE SUCCESSFUL?

I am sure the answer to this question is yes; do you also want to be happy, and again the answer will be yes. Right, stop believing in something that just does not matter and something that does not exist. Go and smash many mirrors, walk around the house with an umbrella up, walk under a ladder and do all the bizarre superstitious stuff there is to do and see what happens. I shall tell you what happens, NOTHING, simple as that, nothing happens because these rituals are just figments of people's imagination created out of ignorance; you need to be better than that.

GET THE MESSAGE

Touch wood, be good, what shit. Now come on, think about it. How many times have you seen people looking around for some wood to touch as if wood has some magical power. Well, these days you would struggle to find a decent piece of wood to touch anyway. In the 1980s when working as a cabinet maker I had the unfortunate experience of working for six years with Disasterville, a cabinet maker by the name of Andy. No manners, no respect, hated everyone, bad-tempered and everything he got involved with became as big a disaster as himself. Whatever he did he messed it up, he was one of life's many Fuck Ups and he was touching wood every day, so what does that tell you?

START TO BE REALISTIC

If you desire to be more confident, and you do, otherwise you would not be reading this book, stop living in the dark ages and be more realistic about what really matters in life. A confident person does not believe in luck, they do not follow any rituals, and they are not superstitious. Later on I shall cover the characteristics of a confident person. As you read my work you will notice that my findings have worked for me and will also work for you. They are simple, your attitude can and will change as you start to concentrate on what really matters and what does not.

There is no secret to becoming confident and it is not difficult. The more you want to be a better person, the more you will find it becomes easier as time goes on and the great advantage is once you have developed a confidence you never had before, it is with you for life, because your mind will only ever think one way. There will be times when you will be down, you will experience all the traumatic situations we all encounter throughout life and you will be upset, suffer emotional heartache and pain, but one thing is true: having your newly developed confidence will help you PICK YOURSELF UP AND DUST YOURSELF DOWN and carry on enjoying life as it comes.

What being confident is, it is your escape plan, it is your get out of jail card, it is your way out of the maze, it is your platinum card to success. When problems happen in my life, and they often do, I do not concentrate on the problem, I only focus my energy on finding the solution. Think of it this way.

You are driving along, and you get a puncture. Unlike in the days when cars carried a spare wheel, as we know today you either have a space saver or a temporary inflation kit. The tyre blows, you pull over where it is safe. If you have breakdown cover you can summon help, or if you feel confident you can attempt to change the wheel.

You cannot find the jack, or the wrench: you eventually find what you need, but the jack is so rusty it won't react, and then you realise you do not have breakdown cover any longer, the spare tyre is flat, and you do not have a pump. You're fucked, and not fucked as you would like to be. Chaotic; does that resemble any aspect of your life?

Confident successful people have everything in order. If your life is not yet in order the real truth is it may never be. From a very young age I have always been neat and tidy and ordered. I know where everything is, I have an amazing filing system. I am reliable.

Personality matters so much in life; when you encounter life's challenges, having that confidence is one of life's best assets and I am sure glad I am me.

CHARACTERISTICS OF A CONFIDENT PERSON

A confident person:

1) Is very relaxed, calmly and clearly spoken.
2) Is self-motivated and comfortable within oneself.
3) Has a high level of personal fitness and wellbeing.
4) Is proud of one's achievements and comfortably speaks openly about them without feeling arrogant.
5) Is happy and comfortable to hear criticism of one's actions and abilities and takes information on board to better oneself.
6) Can comfortably admit to making mistakes and will take positive lessons from them.
7) Can and will speak openly about problems and how they have been overcome.

8) Is willing to praise, encourage and support others.

Confident people are by far the happiest and healthiest of individuals. When they encounter a problem, they quickly address it, looking at positive ways to have the problem resolved. If and when they are down they quickly see the light at the end of the tunnel, and use past experiences to help them quickly overcome their current situation. A confident person will provide you with positive help and encouragement and will always give you good solid advice to help you better yourself for future happiness and wellbeing.

Most confident people are fun to be around, and it can be said that confident people tend to be very intelligent. Do not fall into the trap that intelligence is based on qualifications, far from it. Some of the most intelligent people in the world do not have any great academic qualifications.

The best and most useful of all the qualifications that will help you throughout your life is to have COMMON SENSE, something many people massively lack.

I can tell you this much. If I were trapped in a lift, I would much rather be trapped there with a confident person with common sense than with some academic who lacks the basic skills of life. In my time I have met so many academics who are stupid, no COMMON SENSE and totally fucking clueless.

POINTERS TO HELP YOU

- REMEMBER YOU CANNOT CONTROL EVERYTHING THAT HAPPENS.
- BE REALISTIC WITH YOUR EXPECTATIONS.
- LIFE MAY BE BAD NOW HOWEVER IT WILL BECOME MUCH BETTER IN TIME.
- YOU CANNOT PLEASE EVERYONE SO STOP TRYING.

- STOP BELIEVING IN THINGS THAT SIMPLY DO NOT EXIST.
- HAVE THE COURAGE TO MOVE ON.
- YOU ARE NOTHING WITHOUT COMMON SENSE.

As you continue through my book remember that all things take time and HARD WORK, so be patient and most of all be positive. Start training your mind to be strong, it will not be easy. What you will discover is that it will be worth it. So enjoy the next chapter and as you are now becoming more confident by the day enjoy what you have achieved so far as there are greater things to come.

CHAPTER 4

MOTIVATION

Often we talk of the things we are going to do and achieve, and very rarely do we ever achieve what we once set out to accomplish. Unfortunately it is human nature to be lazy and most people in my experience are. Society has changed somewhat for the better and somewhat for the worse. We now get so much done for us but also expect so much more to be done too, so to be motivated in today's society there just does not seem to be any point, one would think.

WRONG. As human beings our future depends on our motivation. You may not realise it but take for example, two people, one who takes regular exercise and the other who does not. One has to have very strong motivation to do exercises as what one has to put the body through is very unpleasant. However, the end results outweigh any unpleasant feelings experienced. The easy option is to do nothing, and sadly that is the option most people take about life, they just want it easy. Well, life does not work that way if you endeavour to be successful.

When we exercise, our bodies produce endorphins, chemicals in the brain that are responsible for positive moods. The harder we train the more the body produces. The actual exercise we may be doing at that time does not make us feel good, in fact it brings discomfort and a feeling of sheer exhaustion, making us want to stop, but if we push ourselves to a point and complete our set routine, we instantly feel good, and this feel-good factor lasts for a considerable amount of time.

One would hope that doctors are now prescribing exercise to depressed patients as the results are proven. I do not believe in putting chemicals into one's body, I do not take any form of medication. Simply, regular exercise and any form of activity will make us feel much better in ourselves. I train for two hours, five days a week; no excuses unless I am really ill or away working, I train. I have natural motivation because I get results. If you walked up to a fruit machine in an arcade and every time you fed it with coins you won, would you walk away? Same with exercise, put the hours in, put the effort in and you WILL get results. Positive results.

It does go back to what I have said in the past. Easy to say, difficult to do, but not impossible. You MUST be prepared for hard work. That word again, that keeps recurring and for good reason. Hard Work = Positive Results. Motivating oneself, be it to exercise or take up a new hobby or interest, or just to do some gardening or basic housework, is not easy as the easy option is to do nothing or, if one waits long enough, hopefully someone will come along and do it for us.

It amazes me just how useless and lazy most people are; it gives me a massive advantage. If you keep making excuses I WIN. If you keep putting off until tomorrow I WIN. It's raining, I will do it tomorrow, I WIN. I win every time, because I prise my ass off the sofa and I train to make myself the best person I possibly can be. To become a Stuntman I had to be motivated. I would get up at 5am to go to my local riding school and work for three hours to get a free private lesson because I could not afford to pay. I worked, I earned a free lesson. I would be in a cold swimming pool at 7am. On other days I'd be in Ashbourne in Derbyshire sitting on a hill waiting for the weather to be right for my hang gliding qualification.

Night diving at Stoney Cove, Leicestershire for my scuba qualification. Training at gymnastics and fencing in the daytime, trampolining in the evening. It was ruthless, my body was in agony, I never gave up. I was motivated, I was no stranger to hard work, I was 24 and had worked for the past nine years as a cabinet maker and as a joiner on a building site and set up my own cabinet making and joinery business, alongside teaching Kung-Fu, so I knew what hard work felt like.

I was also astute enough to know that if I was going to be a successful Stuntman I had to be prepared for a hard life. So what motivates me? Success. I came from nothing, and I established from a very young age that I needed to change, I needed to be a confident individual to survive life. I hated every second of school. I can see today how the education system and our corrupt government is failing children, and their parents, sadly, are far too stupid to see this.

Education is important, we need to be able to read and write, tell the time, tie our shoelaces, know the days of the week, the months of the year and the seasons; however, very few people know when summer starts and autumn ends and that is appalling.

The education system from comprehensive school and upwards is a complete failure. Our corrupt government is pushing every child into university to keep the unemployment figures down; they graduate with a degree not fit to wipe a tramp's ass with. Our failed education system is creating failures, weak-minded people with no confidence, with low self-esteem, no courage and no bollox, just M.O.D.E.L. 'I have been offended' pathetic children. This is because today children are teaching children; by that I mean teachers are far too young, with no life experience whatsoever, and these so-called teachers are just children themselves, how messed up is that?

You will find more out about what M.O.D.E.L. stands for later in my book.

I was motivated enough to know that by being resourceful and having the drive to succeed I would make it, and no one was going to stop me. To be successful you have to be motivated, you have to be rebellious, and to be a confident person you have to be prepared, as life will not always go your chosen way.

ACCEPT IN LIFE YOU WILL ENCOUNTER KNOCKBACKS

Remember, no one learns to ride a bicycle without experiencing a few falls, even the best riders still take a tumble. Does that mean you have failed? NO. The more ambitious one becomes the more susceptible one becomes to knockbacks. Leave the bike in the shed and you will never fall off; however you will neither progress, become better or ultimately succeed.

As you become more confident you will realise that the knockbacks you encounter along the way are a normal part of life and your motivation to better yourself will override any negative thoughts that may enter your mind.

I cannot make you motivated. Just like giving you confidence, I can only tell you what has worked for me and as you have discovered through previous chapters, I too did lack confidence. Life for me was shit.

I quickly realised that if you want something and want it badly enough you simply have to get up off your lazy ass and work hard to achieve it. You have to MAKE IT HAPPEN. It will not come to you, as simple as that. Just think of the results, even though they could be months or even years away, anything truly worth having in this life is worth working hard for, nothing comes easy. I realised this with both my Kung-Fu training and my stunt training, no one was going to do the training for me and even if they did I still would not benefit, same with learning to drive, you just have to put the time and effort in.

Sometimes it is very hard to motivate ourselves when we are not in full health or are feeling stressed, and just the mere thought of exercise can make us even more reluctant to do anything. When we are feeling low our bodies tend to shut themselves down, mainly to help us relax; we all get down at some point in our lives and when we become stressed we find it hard to see the light at the end of the tunnel.

Just remember, it has taken you some motivation to read this far into my book, and as you have decided, not only are you becoming more confident, you, in turn, are becoming more motivated. Even going for a walk will help, you do not have to run a marathon. Motivate yourself to do something positive. Every little helps.

STRESS

Often people have asked me why I never seem to suffer from stress. The answer is simple: I am on the winning side.

My thought process controls my attitude to life's ups and downs. Basically

Motivation

I have always lived the philosophy that, IF IT HAPPENS IT HAPPENS. This does not by any means mean that I do not have emotions and am not prone to upset, far from it. I experience the same emotions as everyone else. Where I differ is that I experience these emotions but do not suffer them. This is where being strong in motivation comes in. I can always find the positives in any negative situation. I will always motivate myself to act and feel better and you can do the same too. It is a process of thought. I know, no matter what, that life will improve.

I have endured so much negativity in my life and I accept that; however, I will never suffer as I refuse to suffer, I will always find a positive way forward. If I suffer, I become a victim. I am one of life's winners NOT one of life's many losers. If someone can give me a very good reason to worry about problems then I will start to, but no one will ever be able to because simply there are no positive reasons to worry. You have problems in life, worry or solve? Worry or find a solution?

Acknowledging you have a problem is good, worrying about it is bad, and remember once you are feeling stressed and start to worry, your motivation to do the simplest of tasks becomes drained.

The majority of people bring on stress completely by themselves, by trying to fit far too much into one day, arranging to see far too many people and also the fault most people have is trying to please far too many people instead of concentrating on just pleasing themselves.

The importance of being a motivated person works in parallel to being confident, as our first decision to do something new or try a different challenge needs confidence and motivation to work as one. Firstly, the confidence to take up the new challenge and secondly, the motivation to carry it through. You also have to be disciplined. So now you can see the relevance of this chapter.

When you start to see positive results in your ventures, this in itself will make you even more motivated. The same can be said of my writing this book. I had never written a book before. I have the confidence to believe in my work and to know that people will benefit from reading it. What motivates me to write? Firstly enjoyment; I do actually enjoy the work I am putting into this book as I am motivated by the thought of the end result, my first finished book.

I do not have the time to write every day, I motivate myself to do a little each day or, if I am away working, on my return I will concentrate a full day to it. That is discipline. I have found the best way is to always do something rather than nothing and I am the kind of person who likes to plan my week.

An important point, which has been covered so many times before and will be covered again, is that no one is going to do it for you. You have to start to look at the positive results you will achieve by being more motivated and dedicate yourself to being a more positive, confident, motivated and disciplined person. There simply is no magic to it, it is how you play your mind, how far and how fast you want to run. In the following chapter I cover KEEPING YOURSELF MENTALLY STRONG and this chapter is designed to put what you have learned into practice.

IT WORKED FOR ME

Anytime I decided to set a goal, no matter what it may have been, I looked at all the things I have so far achieved, all through dedication and hard work. I remember back in 1987 when I first saw a Lamborghini Jalpa for sale, I wanted one; however, I was realistic enough to know that on a cabinet maker's wage I would never be able to afford one, so I had to change direction.

I need to emphasise a point. Back in 1987 when I saw my first ever Lamborghini I knew if I worked hard and was disciplined, that I would be successful enough to be able to afford one. Now not everyone thinks this way. The second time I went to view it I went with a friend by the name of Tommy. His reaction was completely different to mine; when I said one day I would own a Lamborghini, he laughed and followed his laughter with, we will never be able to afford a car like that. What Tommy was actually doing was projecting his insecurities and his lack of confidence to be successful onto me. I have experienced this insecure behaviour many times: we can't, we won't, we never will.

Because of their lack of drive and discipline to be successful they try to make themselves feel better by including you. Now ironically Tommy never amounted to anything, ending up on the great scrap heap of life with an ugly wife. Again, I won.

Because I believe in myself and know whatever happens I will be successful I can never lose. Growing up I heard the cries of 'get a trade, you will never be out of work'. What no one was saying was that getting a trade as skilful as cabinet making was, sadly, very poorly paid and the number of hours worked was not reflected in the remuneration.

A better life was my motivation to work hard, train hard and eventually become ultra successful and, just to give you an idea of my success, in 2009 I was featured alongside Richard Branson and Bill Gates as one of the most successful businesspeople in the world today. How's that for a boy born in the back streets of Nottingham? Remember, hard work earns us our treats in life. For every hour worked you will appreciate your achievement much more than if you had won it, inherited it, found it, stolen it or even worse, had it bought for you by Daddy.

I can tell you for sure I dated a daddy's girl who received everything she asked for and it was never enough. She ground that pathetic father of hers into the ground, always wanting more and more, and more was never enough for the ungrateful bitch. Until the day she grinds her parents into their graves she will always be the spoilt brat that she is and unfortunately it is such a shame that people can live their lives like a leech, draining others of their wealth. One thing is for sure; her parents were the root of this problem in the first place for constantly spoiling her this way Did she ever thank them? No way, in her small-minded world she felt privileged and expected reward without any natural input from herself.

You will never become self-motivated if you constantly rely on others to carry you throughout your life. If you adopt this selfish attitude, you will eventually come down to earth with one great big bang as the people who are so foolishly carrying you today may not be here to carry you again tomorrow. So beware, if you are a parent who is reading this and thinking, that sounds like my son or daughter, then you need to take a step back and look at your life and why your children lack the motivation to go out and earn their own money instead of sponging off Mummy and Daddy all the time.

So your dream may be to become your own boss: you may be looking at your working life and realising that you are not as happy as you would like to be. Look at the things that make you happy in life. Many people have made very good careers out of hobbies and interests they enjoy and just remember this, when you become your own boss, you very rarely have unhappy days. I became self-employed in 1990, became my own boss, established a very successful career in 1993 as a Stuntman, the rest is history and all because I was motivated.

Whatever your reason for wanting and needing to become more motivated, one thing remains apparent, you will have to be the one to work hard to achieve this and that is exactly what you have to do, WORK HARD, unless your intention is to hope someone will do all the hard work for you. Now is the time to make your plan, think about exactly what you would like to achieve and prepare.

You can read as many self-help, get rich quick, be successful books as you like; however, there is no secret to becoming successful and confident. To put it simply, the secret is hard work.

DO YOUR RESEARCH

Now your ambitions may not be too great. Whatever you desire to be, you first need to look at what is currently causing or preventing you from achieving your goal.

One of the major reasons for people being restricted in their ambition to become more motivated is finance. When I did my research into the cost of becoming a Stuntman I was amazed just how expensive the training was going to be. Now I did not have a very well-paid job and did not have rich parents who could happily fund my training and even if I had, I sure would never have expected them to finance my future.

Of the many abilities I did possess were my skills as a cabinet maker and my ability to work hard, notice that word again, HARD WORK, WORK

HARD. I also looked at all the other skills I had acquired over the years, painting and decorating, bricklaying and also my ability to teach Kung-Fu. So with all these skills I had acquired I set to work to earn the money required to do my stunt training. When I became established with my various instructors it then became apparent that I could work at the stables very early in the morning to earn free riding lessons. This became a great help financially as it allowed me to use the money I was earning to fund the other disciplines which were required.

As you are very well aware, I achieved my goal through self-motivation and went on to gain acceptance onto Equity's elite stunt register, which sadly was dissolved in 2017 after 44 years.

SO WHAT IS HOLDING YOU BACK?

I shall tell you quite plainly and simply exactly what is holding you back: YOU. Yes, like it or not, the only thing that is holding you back right now is you. You are preventing yourself from a better and much more rewarding life. If you are happy with your current situation then cool. If not, stop moaning and feeling sorry for yourself with the mindset that nothing ever goes right for you. Wash these negative thoughts out of your mind right now, as constantly thinking in this most damaging fashion will only grind you even further down the depressive road to failure.

THERE ARE ALWAYS OTHER POSSIBILITIES

As you have just read, I was not a rich kid, and I managed through my own determination to gain all the very expensive qualifications needed to become a Stuntman. One thing I am against is borrowing money. I do not agree with debt. If you want something and you do not have the money, then do without or work hard to earn the money so you can have what you desire. My first vehicle cost me £300 in 1986, which is around £1000 today in 2024. It took me time to save the £300, however my van was mine, no finance, all mine and the best bit, after getting two years' use out of it, I sold it in 1988 for £300.

I worked hard, I saved hard, and I bought what I needed, NOT what I wanted, and I adopt that attitude to this very day.

If you do resort to the loan option, only borrow within your means and if you are reading this book and thinking, I have already borrowed well above my means and need the motivation to pay off my debts, then you need to read on.

Unfortunately for the worst, we live in a world of borrow now and pay back later or never bother to pay back at all. If you have got yourself into financial difficulties, you first need to sit down and look at all of the money you have coming in and then look at all the money you have going out. In many cases we find more goes out than comes in because we just WANT WANT WANT, and we do not think that at some point we are going to have to pay it all back. Borrowing money with no intention of ever paying it back is theft, remember that.

If you are suffering from financial problems, I suggest you first face up to your problem. Never mask any problem with denial; only a coward adopts this foolish attitude. Secondly, start to make sacrifices, only buy what you need, NOT what you want. Do you think you could do that? Stop buying shite from Amazon for a start and cancel that Netflix subscription, you do not need it.

Now there are many self-help books out there for you to read on the subject of debt and this book is designed to make you a more confident person and this chapter is designed to make you motivated. This is another lesson in motivation, go and get yourself a good book to help you straighten out your finances and make sure you read it.

Alongside this book I have written a finance book entitled, From MINI to Millionaire: Want to Get Rich? Without ever borrowing any money? I suggest you read it.

Never fall into the pension trap. I first wrote this book in 2006, some 18 years ago, and since then the world has changed, our country has changed, we are currently in recession. Basically our once-great country is on its sorry ass due to irresponsible 'Shit4Brains' MPs who are not fit to do my washing, as my very good friend Roger put it, fucking up the country. I could go on forever over this. Back to pensions.

What confidence does is, it allows you to believe in yourself, it allows you to be unique and self-sufficient and not reliant on society.

Before I go deep into the workings and failings of pensions, I want you to read and absorb this word, remember I referred to it earlier in this chapter.

M.O.D.E.L. Not a stunner who you would like to nail.

Mediocre

Obedient

Dependent

Entertained

Lifeless

We will come back to the above later.

Pensions were created around the 1700s; by that I mean private pensions, as government pensions do go back further to 1590: the first was to support disabled seamen. I am going to completely separate the government state pension and private pensions.

Originally this is how a private pension functioned.

Workers and individuals paid in at one end, either through a weekly contribution from their wages or by taking out a pension with a provider. This money went into a pot to increase and make money out of the contributors' money, are you following this?

One could draw on their pension from the age of 55, take a lump sum and receive a monthly payout. Life expectancy was predicted that one would be long gone by the age of 75. So for a pension to be successful you first need enough people contributing.

Secondly you need the investment pot to grow. This needs to grow, as this and the people who contribute pay those who have retired, simple as, however, the reality is this.

Not enough people are now contributing. Most cannot afford to and those that do are far too stupid to understand the process. If they studied the principle of how the pension system needs to work they would not get involved. With low interest rates and world instability the pot is not growing, it is actually having the opposite effect and shrinking. One also has to be mindful that fees are deducted from the contributor, these fees pay the provider's employees.

The good news is people are living much longer so have received monthly pension payouts for a duration greater than the structure was originally intended. So to put it to you as directly as I can, I am no Carol Vodaphone, however with my very limited ability with maths I can deduce that the pension system is antiquated.

So why do people still contribute?

Here is your answer.

Because they are just what our corrupt government need them to be. Model citizens.

Mediocre

Obedient

Dependent

Entertained

Lifeless

Are you one of these?

Most people are sheeple: they just follow the crowd and do not have the courage to forge their own way in life. Read the small print. It states clearly that your investment can also lose money, that you may lose part or all of your investment. Today pensions are a gamble I am not willing to take. I do not have one as I do not have any faith in what they now represent.

The government are begging you to invest in one so they can exonerate themselves from all responsibility towards you when you retire and, get a load of this, you get taxed on them, yes, the money you have paid in is taxable. Doomed to fail. If I gave you £50,000, would you like to have full control of it or would you hand it over to a complete stranger to invest it for you?

Control, have the confidence and courage to be in full control of your life. This is my motivation.

IT IS NOT GOING TO COME TO YOU

Stop kidding yourself right now. If you truly want a better life, be happy and confident, you and only you will from this day on have to get up off your backside and make it happen. You will be sitting waiting a very long time if you think that motivation comes to you. It does not happen like that, and it never will. Now someone could constantly bellow at you to get up off your ass and get yourself into a routine, to give you that push you may require, but do remember they cannot and will not be there for you all the time.

I believe there can be no greater motivation than looking around at what others have achieved and believing we can achieve greater things too; remember my decorating story in Chapter One.

Unless you are prepared to put in the many hours of hard work and dedication to reach your chosen goal you may forget about it right now because whatever you aspire to do or be, do not be under any illusion; the only way you will achieve in this life is through many hours of hard work. If you are the kind of person who is lazy and skives away from any form of hard work, be it through employment or exercise, you have two simple options.

- You can stay just the way you are right now and forget about becoming more confident and super successful.
- Or you can stop feeling sorry for yourself, get off your sorry ass right now and start doing something about it.

Constantly moaning and feeling sorry for yourself, filling your mind with negativity and why you cannot do what you most desire to do in life are just foolish excuses for you failing to move from the static position you are in and will always remain in unless you and only you are prepared to begin working hard to make yourself a more positive and confident person.

Now as you are aware, you have motivated yourself in some way to read this far, and as my work begins to sink in many things become apparent about my thoughts and feelings about this subject of motivation. It is not difficult; it is not impossible.

Only you are being difficult with yourself by constantly placing mental barriers in your way, so stop this right now because as you have already noticed life places enough obstacles in our way, and we sure do not need any more to have to climb. Motivating myself in the direction of my goals worked for me, so there is nothing saying that it will not work for you.

NEVER GIVE UP

Never give up. If you really do want to become more confident, to better yourself throughout your life, regardless of what happens to you along the way, do not give up, keep yourself strong. If you follow all the advice given to you throughout my book you can only go one way and that is in a positive direction. Remember, I did not have the advantage of a book like this and there will be times when you will feel low and will lack the motivation you require. This feeling is only temporary, things do get better. So that is why I say, do not give up, keep going, when you feel down today and lack motivation you may not be better tomorrow, keep strong, keep going, DO NOT GIVE UP. When life is ready to give up on you it will let you know.

If you want a better life, you have to be the one to work at it. So do exactly that, Work Hard, get yourself into a routine and you will find motivating yourself becomes a whole lot easier. Life will get better, it always does. I know this because for all the negatives that have happened to me in my life when I adopted the correct mindset and worked on the solution and not the problem, life improved.

In 2009 I dated an amateur model, she was bad news, just tits & fanny, the worst kind, thick as pigshit basically, a Ferrari without an engine. Looked amazing on my arm until she opened her mouth; girls did not understand what I saw in her, guys did.

She was lazy, no matter how much effort I invested in her nothing improved, she was a shit girlfriend, an energy vampire. Motivation, what motivation? She was not prepared to invest in herself and invest in her future, she wanted to be carried throughout her life. She stank of jealousy, insecurity, inadequacy, liability, I could go on and on; as my friends accurately described her, fucking useless.

She would look at all that I had achieved and instead of embracing the fact she was dating Super Successful she resented me. She had to go. Because she was incapable of motivating and improving herself. You have to want it, be hungry for it, work hard for it. If you are not motivated you will fail.

In my excellent chapter, MIXING WITH THE RIGHT KIND OF PEOPLE, I go into more detail about the negatives of having the wrong significant other adversely affecting your life.

POINTERS TO HELP YOU

- GO OUT AND GET IT AS IT WILL NOT COME TO YOU.
- EXERCISE REGULARLY.
- YOU HAVE TO HELP YOURSELF.
- NEVER GIVE UP.
- IF IT HAPPENS IT HAPPENS SIMPLE AS THAT.
- STOP WORRYING IT WILL ONLY WEAR YOU DOWN.

- REMOVE NEGATIVE PEOPLE FROM YOUR LIFE.

Do not waste your time waiting for the perfect moment to arrive, create this moment yourself. I am a firm believer in investing in one's happiness, for being happy is by far the greatest emotion one can feel.

I am happy!

CHAPTER 5

MIXING WITH THE RIGHT KIND OF PEOPLE

Have you ever noticed how someone's words can instantly affect the way we think? All going rather well and then someone happens to say something negative about the way we look or act and despite our strength of character we do get affected by it, or is it just that we allow ourselves to be affected?

WE ALLOW OURSELVES. If you are in the company of positive people on a regular basis you will inevitably become a more positive person yourself. Just think about it, being in the company of a confident person you start to see how they operate, their thought process, how they deal with problems, and you then start to realise that is exactly what they are doing, they are dealing with problems, not running away and hiding from them. Your first observation about a person with a high degree of confidence is that they never have problems for very long. Their ability of dealing with them does not get in the way of the things they like to do most.

The opposite can be said about negative people. The, 'I AM GOING TO FAIL', 'IT WON'T WORK', 'I AM NO GOOD' people. The pessimists. Spend some time around these people and if you do not yet possess the confidence to be one bit affected by their words then they will surely get to you. As you read in the previous chapter, the 'Ferrari without an engine' who I dated in 2009 was all of that.

She was draining; when she was expressing to me that she was no good I should have agreed with her and pushed her out of the door. I would have saved myself a whole lot of trouble.

What I did not realise at the time was that my then girlfriend was a narcissist. Through my journey in life I had never heard of a narcissist so had no idea I had introduced one into my life and how damaging and destructive narcissists are. I really was Sleeping With the Enemy. A friend of mine briefly enlightened me by saying, 'I believe your ex-girlfriend was a narcissist,' as his daughter had suffered at the hands of, as he referred to them, these evil-minded fucks, so that he was certain that I too had been a victim. Sadly he was correct.

After my unfortunate encounter with what I can only describe as Pure Evil I was so fascinated with what I had heard about this mental condition that I wanted to learn everything I possibly could.

I collated information in the form of books on the subject, dedicated hours, days and weeks to reading about the condition on various websites. I watched documentaries, I spoke to experts on the subject of Narcissistic Personality Disorder. What amazed me most was the fact that for the past two years I had had a narcissist as an integral part of my life and never knew this. How would I, never knowing that the condition even existed?

So what is Narcissistic Personality Disorder? If you are not already familiar with the condition what you are about to read is going to shock you, as narcissists are more common than you realise. After reading this chapter I am sure that you will either have dated a narcissist, have worked with, or been employed by one, even have one as a family member or friend. What you are about to read will be the best education of your life to date to protect you from these evil manipulative people. That is exactly what they are, Pure Evil, you are now going to read why.

Firstly, narcissism derives from Narkissos, a mythological Greek young man who became inspired by his own reflection which he saw in a lake. Narcissistic Personality Disorder is a mental condition where the sufferer is in such deep denial that there is anything actually wrong with them that they mirror their unacceptable behaviour onto others, masquerading as the good person while everyone around them in their mind is in the wrong.

Even if, like me, you had never even been made aware of this condition, you will at some point in your life have come into contact with a narcissist.

Interestingly, having studied the condition and having been exposed to a narcissist, I can now identify the condition very easily in others, allowing me a massive advantage, as the way to destroy a narcissist is to expose them. I have been able to help and advise many of my friends, who have also suffered at some point in their life from narcissistic abuse.

So how does a person become a narcissist? Narcissists, male or female, come to fruition in their late teens. Once a person's narcissism has formed they are untreatable, as they are in denial that there is anything wrong with them. NEVER believe anyone who tells you otherwise. Narcissists cannot be treated and cured, it is simply not possible, it is ingrained into their personality and we cannot change our personality once it is formed.

Narcissists are formed from an overbearing mother, a mother who totally idolises their child, fixating in the child's mind that they are so special that they deserve preferential treatment. The real truth is that narcissists are useless socially, they leech off other people's success. Throughout their childhood they have never experienced boundaries, they have always been nurtured to believe they are right no matter what. They become accustomed to constant praise and learn to belittle others, they become expert liars, very deceitful, untrustworthy, and master manipulators.

Symptoms of Narcissistic Personality Disorder:

- Has a grandiose sense of self-importance, exaggerates achievements and talents, expects to be recognised as superior without clear achievements.
- Is preoccupied with fantasies of unlimited success, power, brilliance, beauty, or love.
- Believes that he or she is 'special' and unique' and can only be understood by, or should associate with, other special or high-status people or institutions.
- Requires excessive constant admiration.
- Has a very strong sense of entitlement. Unreasonable expectations of especially favourable treatment, expecting others to comply with their expectations.

- Is exploitative of others, regularly takes advantage of others for their own gratification.
- Lacks empathy, is totally unwilling to recognise or identify with the feelings and needs of others.
- Is often envious and jealous of others, delusionally believing that others are envious or jealous of them.
- Arrogant, disrespectful behaviour or attitudes towards others.

So there you now see what a person is up against, dating, working, sharing a life with someone with Narcissistic Personality Disorder.

Throughout my life, from school until this day, I have had my dealings with awkward people, some nasty, some very evil, some stubborn, some very dishonest. I have, however, never encountered such unacceptable behaviour as that of a narcissist. They are like nothing I have ever encountered in my life. This personality is dangerous and needs to be avoided at all costs.

Easier said than done. Why, you ask. Because narcissists are experts at masking their true personality until they have trapped you and that is exactly what they do, they in time make you believe that it is not possible for you to function without them. Narcissists can only survive with narcissistic feed, that is why they are often referred to as energy vampires. When you come into contact with a narcissist they are assessing if you are susceptible to their unconventional behaviour.

So for myself, being a very relaxed, easy going, very forgiving guy, I was the perfect bait for a stunning female narcissist. In the first two weeks of any relationship, both males and females are on their best behaviour, which is normal. After two weeks our true personalities begin to show, and it is then that the narcissist sets out to work on you. Slowly through time narcissists are manipulating your mind. They are expert infiltrators; this is about the only skill they actually possess, as destructive as it becomes.

If you continue a relationship with a narcissist one of three things WILL happen, not may happen, they WILL in time happen, they are as follows.

1) You will eventually kill the narcissist.

2) You will go insane.

3) You will kill yourself.

There is no happy ending to being in a relationship with someone with Narcissistic Personality Disorder, they are destructive. For myself, now knowing what I was dealing with made a massive difference to how I was now going to handle my ex. The best way to defeat your enemy is to educate yourself about your enemy, how and why they think in a certain way, their irate unpredictable behaviour.

What I then proceeded to do was learn everything about this very unusual condition so I was in the strongest possible position to defeat her. For the past two years she had slowly drained me of my energy and was also destroying the strong personality that I am, through her own inadequacies and insecurities.

So how many people out there are narcissists today? More than you realise.

Female narcissists tend to use charm, whereas male narcissists tend to be very aggressive like a bull, although female narcissists can be very nasty and aggressive when they are confronted and exposed. It is their form of defence. Because of what could be described as a new style of parenting, one where the child appears to control the parent, not the other way around, you are going to encounter more narcissists than ever before.

If you examine 'learned behaviour', where a child has never been set any boundaries, where certain parents are fucking clueless, blaming everyone else for their inadequacies, they will blame anyone but themselves for the total fuck-up of a child or children that they drag up into this world. Children copy, so when they see a parent behaving in such a manner, they know no better than to copy unless a parent is intelligent enough to prevent this mirroring at an early stage. With narcissists the mother tends also to be a narcissist, so what chance has the child got? Very little, as they inevitably will become narcissists too.

Narcissistic Personality Disorder is not detected until adult life, where it can clearly be seen that the adult is using childish traits to get its own way. The body has developed into an adult, but unfortunately the brain has not and still reverts to its childish ways to get what it wants. Think child having a tantrum in the supermarket because it wants sweets and it wants them now; what does the inadequate parent do? Lavishes the spoilt brat with exactly what it demands, so the child relates bad behaviour with a positive reward.

What happened to the days of sending the little fucker down a coal mine? So there you have it, an insight into Narcissistic Personality Disorder. What you will now find is that you yourself reading this will either be a narcissist or have been the victim of one, more probably know a narcissist or have been a victim, as most narcissists won't be bothered to read a self-help book unless it was actually about them.

What narcissists are expert at is manipulating situations to make themselves look more successful than they actually are; they thrive on other people's success. That is why when you have reached a very high level of success, like me, and coupled with that you are a very relaxed cool personality, you are easy prey for these energy vampires. Just like a vampire needs a constant supply of blood, a narcissist thrives on drama and the disruption they cause to other people's lives. Narcissists are unable to be reasonable, they are not diplomatic, or considerate, they are pure evil. You MUST avoid them!

Never allow anyone to manipulate you. This is exactly what our government does, they try and sometime succeed in manipulating people, they could never manipulate me, I am far too smart for them.

Sometimes it can be rather difficult to avoid being around manipulative people; you may be unfortunate to work with one or even worse, work with a group of them. I once did and my way out was to first tell myself, IT IS ONLY TEMPORARY, I will not be working for this company for life, and to turn their negative attitude around on them and use humour to combat their negative influences on myself and others.

Mixing with the Right Kind of People

As I have mentioned earlier in my book and I shall keep reminding you, the thoughts that enter your mind, either good or bad, are put there by one person and one person alone, YOU, simple as that.

Think of all the amazing achievements man has successfully produced over time. Now think of the negative conversations that developed through these ideas and visions, that never put off the inventors, creators, designers, great minds; it only inspired them even more to prove people wrong.

I refer to this as FUEL FOR MY FIRE. When I decided to train to become a Stuntman I received constant negative words from so many people. Every time a person responded in a negative manner it made me even more determined to succeed. It was the best form of motivation I could have ever received, it allowed me the satisfaction of being able to prove so many people wrong and I did.

It is never difficult in life to work out the good from the bad, to understand the ones who will support you and show you encouragement and belief. It becomes very easy to establish the people who would be so happy to see you fail, basically because they are far too lazy to get off their ass and achieve something worthwhile for themselves.

It becomes so apparent when in a situation you plan to do something and you hear the words from others saying, "You will never do that." The reason people say these things is a true reflection of themselves. What they are really saying is that they lack the confidence and motivation to do what you are thinking of and planning.

If you are negative, you are not for me. I am ruthless, I remove you from my life.

Human nature can sometimes prove itself to be very easy to work out. Very few people have the courage to do what they really would like to do in life and then when you come along and say, "I have decided I am going to run a marathon this year," the negative words start to fly in your direction in droves, basically from the ones who would love to have the courage and confidence to do exactly what you have decided to do.

With Confidence

Everyone suddenly has a reason why you should not run a marathon.

At the beginning of 1990 I realised sadly that I had to leave six years of working at Thomas Pearson behind me, as I just was not earning enough. The girlfriend at the time was unsupportive and I could see why; her parents were Negs. Negative about their life, your life and everyone's life. They tried to place every form of negativity for starting my own business into my mind and that failed, because I looked at their shit house lives and thought, are you a business mentor? Are you a good ambassador that I need to learn from?

They lived in Shitsville, were in debt, shit shape, shit life, going nowhere fast. I was going to establish my new cabinet making and joinery business no matter what they thought. Ironically it was my then girlfriend who made an issue of me earning less than her. To put it into context, I earned £105 per week in 1990 and she earned £135 for doing fewer hours as an office clerk and there was I, a skilled craftsman; that is how messed up England was even back then. As we know it is more messed up than ever today.

So never be put off by their negative words of discouragement or you will forever regret not doing what you so wanted to do. Use all their negativity positively and throw even more fuel on your fire of adventure and may it keep burning strong and hot, encouraging you onto even greater goals.

A very important message regarding your response to negativity: never be rude or bad-mannered or get angry towards these people; remember, no matter how much you disagree with them you will never change their mindset, only they can do that. If they want to continue being negative and having the world constantly fall apart around them, just simply walk away and leave them to it, blank them out of your mind, move on and you enjoy better things, they are insignificant. As you have already discovered so far, being confident and positive brings you far more benefits than being negative and pessimistic. The most important commodity you will achieve is true happiness, next to our health the most important possession in all our lives. Remember the reasons for reading this book are for your benefit and not for you to try and change other people or to dictate to them about their chosen way of life.

I write my words hard, I write my words aggressive for good reason, because they have the desired impact. Read most other so-called self-help books, they are SHITE. I write with meaning and honesty, and I have a pedigree to prove it. How many so-called self-help book authors can say that?

It is very important now as you have read this far to start to develop your communication skills to benefit your life. As you become more confident, your ability to communicate with others becomes more apparent as you start to feel much better within yourself. It is also quite true that as we age, we do become more confident within ourselves. This is purely down to life's experiences and development of knowledge and better understanding of life.

WE CAN ALL LEARN SOMETHING FROM EACH OTHER

Regardless of an individual's level of confidence, or intelligence for that matter, from spending time with anyone positive or negative we can all learn something. I am a great communicator; however I find people who lack a great sense of humour can sometimes be a struggle to get along with. I have the aptitude to get on very well with anyone, however I find it easier to accept that not everyone shares my style and it becomes much easier to just walk away before you begin to realise your humour can be misinterpreted as offensive. Unfortunately, and through no fault of our own, some people do take unnecessary offence to the most trivial of matters. Remember, insecure people can be very sensitive.

When I came into the world of stunts I thought that my colleagues would share and appreciate good humour; how wrong I was. I found most of the Stuntman and Stuntwomen I associated with were just not my kind of people. They were negative, cowardly, yes you read that correctly, cowards. Lacked any form of ambition, again which surprised me because television and film are ambitious industries.

Some people just do not get it, and if you and they do not get along no matter how hard you try, it always seems that if you have confidence and a great sense of humour that the conversation is always one-sided and if you were to stop talking then there would be dead silence. I found this so often around stunt people, not my kind of people, my coping strategy a very easy one, I do not have to live with them. I would keep my association with them to an absolute minimum.

This has happened to me so many times. I now accept that not everyone is as happy and cheerful as me. I do not mix with these people, and they do not mix with me, simple as that. Conversation and the ability to communicate with one another is a natural part of life and being human. So if you find yourself in a situation where you are the one keeping the conversation alive, try this, stay silent until they speak and if they do not have anything to say, interesting or not, then they are not the kind of people you need to be socialising with, because simply conversation needs to be two ways, if they are not prepared to make some effort then why should you.

It is by no means that I have a low level of tolerance for quiet people, it is that we are born to communicate and born to shine, and I like to talk, it is how we learn. If I ask someone a question, I expect them to ask one back or at least give something more than a yes or no answer. If you like silence go and live in a monastery, remember, you are a long time dead so make the best of what you have been given and use it to your greatest advantage, you will day by day develop into a very intelligent and interesting person. I worked with negative 'going nowhere fast' kind of people as a cabinet maker from 1984 until 1990. I never allowed them to affect me, no matter what, I was going to be successful.

Try surrounding yourself with positive successful individuals, ones who have a story to tell. I enjoy hearing about people's success and how they achieved great wealth. I know what it was like to be broke, to be poor, to have nothing, to be cold and hungry. I knew there was more for me in life, I read books, listened to cassettes of very successful people's journeys. Yes, when most lads my age were listening to music while they drove, I was listening to motivational speakers, successful businessmen who inspired me.

I stood outside in the pouring rain looking into supercar showrooms, knowing that one day I would succeed. I never had the right kind of

Mixing with the Right Kind of People

people around me. I did not know anyone who was super successful, and I still made it, no internet to inspire me, just that strong desire to better myself. Do remember that you must never let anyone grind you down to their level. If they lack confidence, intelligence and humour then that is their problem. If you have to mix and communicate with these people, make it as brief as you possibly can.

So what have you learned so far? You know that by being around positive people you will become positive, you also know that being around negative people, unless you are very strong-minded, inevitably they will make you a negative and miserable person just like themselves, so try your best to keep well away from these people. Limit your association if you do have to mix with them. Get yourself a great set of friends, ones with a great sense of humour and a positive outlook on life, and you will never go far wrong.

If it means having few or no friends that is much better than having an army of negativity draining the life out of you. If my friends do not bring value to my life they are gone; as you know I am ruthless, I do not need friends to function. However, if you become one of my friends you are part of the elite, you will be a very special person.

Enjoy what you have learned so far. Now get ready for what is coming next.

POINTERS TO HELP YOU

- ONLY MIX WITH POSITIVE PEOPLE.
- KEEP YOUR ASSOCIATION WITH NEGATIVE PEOPLE AS BRIEF AS POSSIBLE.
- NEVER ALLOW ANYONE TO GRIND YOU DOWN AND CONTROL YOUR MIND.
- REMAIN FOCUSED ON YOUR GOALS AT ALL TIMES.
- EDUCATE YOURSELF, REMEMBER KNOWLEDGE IS YOUR BEST DEFENCE.

Remember as time goes by your true friends will always be there for you and there will be times you will feel lonely but remember, as things happen in life, friends will come and friends will go. True friends, however, will be there with you for life.

You are much better being around very few positive people than being surrounded by droves of negative individuals who drain you of all good feeling, like leeches. You have so far invested quality time into the readings of my book, and you have found that you are a more confident and happier person than you were before you started to read it. So do remember what I have said, DO NOT ALLOW NEGATIVE PEOPLE TO GRIND YOU DOWN. You are the one in control, not them.

Just think, how many negative people would actually invest the money and time to read this book? Positive people will.

CHAPTER 6

TURNING A NEGATIVE EXPERIENCE INTO A POSITIVE ONE

Often in life we will experience negative situations and, as you have already read, we now know how to CONTROL THE UNCONTROLLABLE. What we also need to be able to do is look back at all negativity, learn from these unfortunate experiences and turn them around to help you better your future by only seeing these events as TEMPORARY SETBACKS.

As you are now aware from my writing, I am not the kind of person who will ever let anything get me down for long, I am very resilient and do recover from setbacks very quickly without too many scars. When you get to your fifties it can be said you are one of 'the walking wounded'. My analogy to my mindset is a thought process I have developed which works very well for me and will also work well for you too: I call it, SNAKES AND LADDERS.

Simply play a game of snakes and ladders and see if you can get to the end of the game without going down any snakes. The same can be said about life; no way are you going to go through your whole existence without some kind of emotional, physical or psychological problem, it is just not possible owing to the unpredictability of life.

Remember, being confident will not make you immune to the emotional difficulties and traumatic experiences life can sometimes throw at us. Being confident will rapidly help you overcome these problems and get you back on track to a better life.

With Confidence

Remember SNAKES AND LADDERS. Everyone at some point in their life will experience some kind of emotional problem because we are only in control of ourselves and our own minds, not other people's, so inevitably problems are going to arise as we are not always going to agree.

Now get that SNAKES AND LADDERS board out, you have something to try. Just before you do, a short history of the oldest board game in the world. Originating in India, referred to as Moksha Patam, it serves as a moral teaching tool about the good and evil deeds in life.

I have a handcrafted board on display in my home as a reminder of my journey through life, which my fiancée bought me. Put your counter on start and only you play. Throw the dice and see if you can get to the finish without sliding down any snakes.

I have applied this theory to life; when you land on a snake and slide down, do you leave the game and walk away? In crude terms, do you end your life? Fortunately, very few people choose this option. Most people will take a step back and from the outside looking in, will look at all of the good things they have achieved so far in their lives and will discover that to achieve so much, one will have to have suffered at some point some emotional distress and hardship.

So how did you get from being low to high to low again, it happens. Maybe through time, an uncontrollable factor. The fact is, if you were at an all-time low before and managed to pick yourself up, you can and will get yourself back again.

Since first writing this book in 2006 I have encountered many lows, ironically always from relationships, see why, mixing with 'the right kind of people' is vital.

I also had a problem with over 3000 houses being built right opposite my peaceful residence ruining my home life. I went from liking where I lived to absolutely hating it, with Shitsville being constructed opposite and 'not my kind of people' moving in, it sure did turn the area into a slum, did it get me down? Yes, it did. Did I allow it to consume me? No, what I did was realise that I was never going to prevent the build. I could, however, be disruptive, and believe me I was, the developers hated me, and I loved every second of it. I enjoy being hated and do you know why? Because when people hate me, I know I am doing well, as most people hate to see success.

One of my many sayings is:

The Only Taste of Success Some People Get is When They Try to Take a Bite Out of Me.

I turned a negative experience into a positive one by putting my house on the market and relocating to a stunning hamlet deep in the countryside, surrounded by 'my kind of people'. As shitty and uncomfortable as the whole experience was, it pushed me in a direction I would not normally have gone.

What did I learn from one bad relationship after the other? I finally established what I did not need, I did not need parasites, losers, users and fakes. So when looking for a life partner I was focusing more on what I wanted and needed and seemed to always end up with 'tits & fanny', again those badly serviced Ferraris without engines.

I looked back at the stronger aspects of my life, how successful I was as a Stuntman and as a businessman, taking myself from nothing to someone. I established that I needed a strong woman, one who was also successful in her own right, not the parasites, losers, users and fakes I had been attracting. Life can be a barrel of shit at times and one wonders, is this actually happening to teach me a lesson? Life is one big school. I was never going to allow those negative events in my life to control me. I control me. I have learned so much from life and at the time of writing this I am only 56 and I have achieved great success, I have experienced both good and bad. No matter what happens to me I have the confidence to know IT IS ONLY TEMPORARY.

Have I learned? I sure have; the most powerful lesson I can give you is to establish not what you want, establish what you do not want.

JUST ANOTHER BRICK IN THE WALL

The more bricks you build into your wall the stronger your wall becomes. Not only will your wall be stronger, it will also be substantial, stand up to the elements and endure the test of time. Each day, build more confidence into your life, just as you would adding bricks to your wall.

Adapt the above to your life. As you have read and absorbed my writings you have so far established how to become a more confident person. You now are making your life that much better and stronger: or are you? Remember SNAKES AND LADDERS. Pick up the dice, only you can realise you have to move on by picking up that dice, you have motivated yourself to a more positive and confident life.

On many occasions in my late teens, as you are now aware, I purchased bad cars; I never seemed to learn, one bad car after the other. I was given good advice many times and told to walk away but I wanted the car so badly I decided to take my chances at my own expense. This only came to an end after saving for two years to buy an impressive car as I did not and still do not believe in getting loans. If you cannot afford it, then do not have it. If you want it badly enough, work hard and save for it, and that is exactly what I did: unfortunately for me I saved hard and then bought another bad car.

It was a BMW, which had very good interior and exterior, the paperwork all looked in order and the price was very reasonable. However, I was told to walk away from this car as something just did not seem right and only two months later it all became apparent why. The camshaft broke on the car and the repair bill was far too expensive for me to afford, so the car was sold at a great loss to me. Well, I certainly learned my lesson from this one and by no means do I ever regret buying that car, as that one experience taught me such a good lesson at a young age.

I had learned something very valuable from that experience and sometimes in life you do have to take chances and go with your instincts. In my case, I took my chances and all failed to the extent that the most important point to come from this is A LESSON LEARNED.

Turning a Negative Experience into a Positive One

So when will we stop learning and start living without making these mistakes? We will never stop making mistakes, we may not make the same mistakes again as hard lessons learned are never forgotten, but as we mature we do tend to be a little wiser and not fall foul of something that would have earlier tripped us flat on our face. So remember, when you do make mistakes, if you are able to take a positive message away from the experience you have DEVELOPED A POSITIVE ATTITUDE TO LIFE.

So do not beat yourself up too hard because you seem to never learn. You are learning all the time. I have heard it said many times that YOU WILL NEVER STOP MAKING MISTAKES UNTIL THE LAST NAIL IS DRIVEN INTO YOUR COFFIN.

Accept that is how life is. WE LIVE AND LEARN from our mistakes, there is always something we can salvage from a bad experience. I have a neighbour who is incapable of taking good advice. I tried to help him, however, due to his deep-rooted insecurities he thinks that taking good advice means he is a failure. Well to be fair he is a failure, however that is a different book.

When you were shown how to tie your shoelaces, learn the days of the week, tell the time, there is a correct way and many wrong ways, no matter what positive advice my neighbour is presented with he will not take it on board and aborts yet another job. A job done right that takes a person willing to listen; two hours and five days later he is still fucking himself and the job up.

Those kinds of people never learn. Life's fuck-ups; the only thing they are good at is being shit! I just do not have time for these kinds of people.

As you have learned from 'mixing with the right kind of people', being around the wrong kind of people will have a negative impact on your life and can mess with your thought process. Surround yourself only with positive people, this will create feeling more confident within yourself and very rarely now will you think in a negative manner.

IF IT IS GOING TO HAPPEN IT IS GOING TO HAPPEN, simple as that, so do not bother yourself and other people with these negative thoughts of problems and events that simply may never happen. If they do unfortunately happen, direct your energy into your problems or difficulties when it is required, not now when you should be enjoying happier times.

There are enough 'what ifs' in this world, we do not need any more, so do not be one. By thinking positively you will continually develop a happier attitude towards your life even on your worst days.

My bad days are much better than most people's good days.

Remember what you read in the introduction about me: I was a very shy person, lacked confidence and lacked the motivation to better myself because I was always telling myself I would never be good at anything. I practically convinced myself of this and as you now know it was participating in Kung-Fu, to which I owe the best time of my life, that changed me. I wanted to change, because I just sat and watched everyone else having a great time and lacked the confidence to go out there and be the best that I could possibly be.

I made the decision to better myself and it worked, I made myself confident through developing a more positive thought process to my life. I knew it would not be easy and believe me, it has not been an easy journey, however it is the most rewarding journey I could have ever travelled and am still travelling on that journey today, all thanks to developing CONFIDENCE. Deciding that yes life can and will be hard, also very difficult to understand, however by thinking only of the good I will achieve and training my thoughts that any setbacks I encounter will only be TEMPORARY. To achieve greater things in life, I have to accept that I will experience setbacks along the way, however the rewards will be worth it.

You may, as you read this, have a problem that you need to overcome. Normally we do not consider reading self-help books until we need to, just like we never bother to check the tool kit in our cars until we are

Turning a Negative Experience into a Positive One

stranded on a dark country road in the pouring rain and we then discover we are missing the jack.

I too, am guilty of this. I have read many self-help books long after the event and had wished I had only bothered to pick these books up sooner. However, when everything is going well in your life the last thing you think of is reading a book to make your life better when your life is great as it is. It is true that we only read this kind of book when an event prompts us to. You are reading one now; when future events occur you will have that extra advantage of being mentally and physically stronger to deal with it.

A very important fact and one that should never be overlooked is always face up to your problems. Do talk to people you feel comfortable with as this will help you try to understand better your own thoughts and feelings. It is very rare that in adult life we will not all have experienced some form of emotional upheaval; remember we are 'the walking wounded'.

Ultimately it must be you and you only who makes the final decision as to which direction your life travels in. Yes, do listen to good advice and take all opinions on board, you are the one who has to live with the consequences and what you do not want to happen is you start to blame others because you did more of what they wanted you to do than that which your own mind was telling you.

Other people can and do have a strong influence on our thoughts and our behaviour. When we look at children who have been the victims of bullying, many years later after the events have gladly come to a close, they still bear the mental scars and do become very withdrawn and sometimes aggressive themselves. It is difficult to stand by your thoughts when everyone seems to be directing you down what you believe to be the wrong path. Well, if you are giving it some thought that is good, as even if you decide to do things your way and their way was right, at least you had the confidence to believe in yourself and you will have learned another valuable lesson.

Remember what you have read about pensions. Why are people still so shit stupid to invest in them? If you are smart, by the time you retire you should be independent. There are far better ways to invest your money today than trusting in an antiquated system. I hear it so many times, our corrupt government saying, invest in a pension, they even created the workplace pension trap that forces you in and you have to opt out and they make it nearly impossible to do that. Money that you have earned today taken and invested into a pension will never be seen again.

If you do not want your earnings that badly I will have them, I love money.

Just as they did with the workplace pension, they did the very same with organ donation. Instead of allowing the individual to make the choice, everyone now is automatically stripped of their vital organs before you have even hit the ground and most people are so stupid they do not even know this.

I opted out on the very first day, Fuck 'em, they ain't getting any of me. It amazes me how so many people just sleepwalk through life totally clueless. I will reiterate, the government wants you to be their slave, their bitch, remember, M.O.D.E.L.

That is exactly what the government needs you to be, the government does not want strong confident people because they cannot control that kind of personality.

If you are a model citizen you are well and truly fucked, there is no hope for you.

Be strong!

Just as you keep your body strong, you need to keep your mind strong, too. Do not get too deeply involved in negative thoughts, you can dilute these thoughts away very easily, just look back at all you have achieved to date; was it through negative thinking that made you what you are today? No, so stop being negative, stop thinking doom and gloom, start to laugh more, look back to your childhood, look at the way children play. One thing about our society which I strongly disapprove of is that we are being made to grow up far too quickly.

There is plenty of time to be a responsible adult and even as one you can still laugh and see the good in life and the good in some people, yes, there are some good people out there, it is a shame that good people are a rarity. That is the way this world is. I cannot change people nor can you, they have to change themselves and have to want to change for the better.

POINTERS TO HELP YOU

- LOOK AT SETBACKS AS ONLY TEMPORARY.
- REMEMBER THE SNAKES AND LADDERS THEORY.
- THERE IS ALWAYS SOMETHING WE CAN SALVAGE FROM A NEGATIVE EXPERIENCE.
- FOCUS YOUR ENERGY INTO WHAT IS ACTUALLY HAPPENING, NOT WHAT MAY HAPPEN.
- YOU ARE HUMAN AND YOU WILL ALWAYS MAKE MISTAKES.
- USE EACH MISTAKE AS A LEARNING EXPERIENCE.
- THE FINAL DECISION IN LIFE IS YOUR DECISION.
- YOU ARE RESPONSIBLE FOR YOUR OWN THOUGHTS AND ACTIONS.

There are times when we sometimes think situations will never get any better than this, we are feeling down and lack the strength to motivate ourselves into positive thinking. Do remember all our experiences in life, good and bad, are there for all of us to build on.

Be the best person you possibly can be. You are the one in control. You may be feeling down at present, not for long though, as you now read on you are developing confidence and positivity to help you deal with the challenges of life.

CHAPTER 7

THERE IS MORE THAN ONE PEBBLE ON THE BEACH

So your relationship has ended, the boss simply had enough and now you are unemployed, it happens. Unfortunately throughout our whole lives you and I will both experience highs and lows. Are we going to let the past have such a strong hold on our future that we are going to dwell in self-pity about issues that now have happened? Even the most pessimistic of people would know we cannot turn back the clock.

Do not for one moment get me wrong. I do understand that certain problems in your life are not to be taken lightly. We all experience emotional upset which can really set us back. If we did not have a natural reaction to any form of rejection or bereavement we just would not be functioning normally. It does not matter how strong a person you are or how tough you think you can be, it is not possible not to be somewhat affected by personal problems.

The shock factor in these situations can be incredible. We experience several emotions from tearful moments to many sleepless nights, anger and loss of appetite. Whatever your situation, the first thing you need to do is accept it has happened. For whatever reason it did. For many weeks, months, even years, situations can still affect us. As I have stated, you are not the first person to have experienced this and you sure will not be the last.

So how are we going to move on and look to our future in a more positive manner? Well, just like this.

Now you have accepted the situation, you are going to keep yourself busy, whether it be through work, a hobby, or socialising with friends. Think of the things you really enjoy doing in life or something you considered doing and never got around to. Now is your chance, get yourself out there and keep that mind occupied. The more your mind is channelled into being active, the less you will be thinking about your situation.

Anytime you feel down, do talk to friends, family or someone you feel at ease with. The worst thing you can do is to hold back your feelings and emotions like some kind of mental torture towards yourself. Get yourself out and explore, walk through the countryside, drive, play music. You know the activities you like to do best, so when you are ready go and do them.

Confidence is not a protection against emotional upheaval. What it does do, though, is help you recover rapidly and help you back to your normal routine.

We have never been failed so much as a society; our corrupt government tries to control us, this has led to resentment and anger, alongside life's problems we now have to deal with all the shit the government tries to dole out towards us and that is the number one reason depression is so high today, all caused by our thoughtless, selfish, pathetic government.

When problems arrive in my life, I do have a much better approach and attitude in dealing with them than when I lacked confidence. The saying, 'there is more than one pebble on the beach' is so true and my mindset follows this pattern on a regular basis. I just know whatever happens, happens. I will endure, be stronger and a much happier person.

When people say, "Things happen for a reason", they do not happen for a reason, they just happen. Simple as that. We do know why certain things in life happen to us. Death is the direction in which we are all heading from the second we are born. Do not waste valuable time and energy wondering why a certain event happened to you, accept it, that is the uncontrollable nature of life sometimes. Things happen to us all, some very good, some very bad. What you need to be able to do is have a strong belief that things will get better and this will come much easier to you when you develop more confidence within yourself.

I very rarely get down; nothing really ruffles my feathers. It is not that I have a 'could not care less' attitude, it is more that I do realise life has its problems and the nature of life is that if you expect the unexpected and never expect too much, you will be travelling along the winning road. You know what works for you. Anytime problems come my way, and believe me they do, I just tell myself, they are ONLY TEMPORARY, and it will not be long before everything is cool again.

Never get into the habit of concerning yourself with why a certain person said or did a particular thing. All you will do is drive yourself crazy over things that simply do not matter. Just look at how messed up this country is today, in 2024, with political correctness, far too many people being far too sensitive. Are you really going to be one of those sad pathetic people who drags themselves through life feeling offended?

I just hate everyone equally, it's much easier that way.

I have a real admiration for Oliver Cromwell. I am an atheist, and later on in my book I shall explain why. Oliver Cromwell was a very religious man, what he did made its mark on history. He had a belief; now whether he was right or wrong is not the issue here. He believed so much in himself and believed he could change the country for the better and had the courage to stand by those beliefs. He is a fine example of a man of confidence. What he set out to achieve, he did.

On 30 January 1649 Charles I was executed. One of the signatories of his death warrant was Oliver Cromwell. After that day England became a republic and has remained that way ever since. Now you may say, well we have a King Charles III but he is only king by title, he has no power whatsoever, our corrupt government has the power. Oliver Cromwell became Lord Protector, head of England, this was a man of courage, confidence and self-belief. He did exactly what he set out to do.

Now how many times have you heard someone say, "I am going to do … " and they never do. Nothing comes to you easy in this life, you have to be the one who goes out there and makes it happen. Change things for the better. So if things are not quite going the way you would like them to, you have to be the one to be brave enough to make the decision to make things better and then get out there and make the change.

Another fine example of someone who 'made it happen', who also had self-belief, who ironically was laughed at, was Nigel Farage. A truly confident man. He believed in himself, he believed in his vision to remove us from the European Union, he forced a referendum, he was successful, we voted LEAVE. He won, now that takes confidence. As Nigel says, who's laughing now?

I know from experience that it will not come to you.

You are the one in control of your future, you decide how fast and how far you are prepared to run. Train yourself to think positively By thinking positively this will help you to become confident and mentally strong.

SETTING GOALS

Shooting at the target, keep firing and you will eventually hit the bullseye. Put the weapon down, walk away, you will never achieve a dead hit.

Easy to say, difficult to do, BUT NOT IMPOSSIBLE.

If your life is just not going in the direction you would like it to go, then do something about it. When I decided I wanted better things in life, I went out there and worked very hard to better myself. I am so pleased that I had the confidence and courage to terminate my employment as a cabinet maker, as the company I then worked for went into liquidation in 1995 due to lack of new contracts, leaving several skilled craftsmen unemployed.

I know from my own experience exactly what it can be like. You are sitting there thinking, I would so much like to do ... or now thinking back, I wish I had done ... Do not be sitting there in a year or more just thinking, you have to take action and MAKE A PLAN.

Remember what you have just read about firing at the target, you have already read the chapter about motivation. Ultimately you would like your life to be much happier, you would like to be much healthier, these things are easily achieved once you change the way you think and start thinking more positive thoughts by motivating yourself towards better things and ultimately you will, as you already are finding, you are becoming confident as the days go by.

You may hear people say, an individual is 'overconfident'. Not possible, it is simply not possible to be overconfident. You are either confident or not, simple as that. You develop your confidence through life's experiences, however no way will you ever have more confidence than you need. You will constantly build upon what you have already developed, and you will day by day become a much stronger person; you will notice yourself just how much your life will change when you doubt yourself much less than you did before.

So now your mind has been supplied with more confidence, for now you are thinking of the things you so much planned to do, but never did, so now is your time to go and MAKE IT HAPPEN.

You can read self-help book after self-help book, they are all helpful to an extent. The real test is not what is contained in the many books out there, it is what you have absorbed into your mind and what applies to you, and you alone. Take all my help and advice that you have now absorbed into your mind, keep going over various chapters if you feel the need, apply this to your everyday life and see just what happens

A very important point: BE POLITE. There are far too many rude, arrogant, selfish, self-centred people out there, do not become one of them. These are the very people who destroy themselves. Yes, they will be jealous of you, who cares? They simply do not matter. You matter, they do not, they are insignificant.

Read MIXING WITH THE RIGHT KIND OF PEOPLE again if you wish.

I just do not have any time for rude people; as far as I am concerned if they cannot be respectful and have something as simple as good manners then I do not want to be in the company of such people. A friend of mine summed these individuals up very well with the saying, "They are people who are going nowhere in life very fast", and how true those words are.

They have a 'bad attitude' problem.

Some things in your life will take considerable time and hard work to achieve. I know very well through my training to become a cabinet maker, then my constant Kung-Fu training, to the many hours of pain endured to become a Stuntman. It is far from easy. I wanted to be a cabinet maker, I wanted to do Kung-Fu and most of all I wanted to be a Stuntman. I knew through hard work I would be successful.

I have achieved exactly what I set out to do. Even when others doubted me, I still believed in myself and developed such confidence that I became immune to negative views and criticism from others. When sometimes in life bad things happen to me, yes, I do get upset, this is my natural emotive state, I too am human, just like you. I just do not stay down for very long; I do not mope around feeling sorry for myself. Once I have acknowledged the problem, I then move on to finding a solution and yes, there always is one out there. Now you are seeing the strong relevance to this chapter, as I say:

THERE IS MORE THAN ONE PEBBLE ON THE BEACH.

I look back at leaving my employment as a cabinet maker and now working since 1993 as one of the world's most successful Stuntmen.

I think back to the many parasitical girlfriends that I had the displeasure of dating, they will all be on the scrapheap of life now, just the next guy's shag and a shit shag at that.

They are now another guy's problem, thankfully not mine. I have an amazing fiancée now.

Life just keeps getting better and better and do you know why?

Simply because I MAKE IT HAPPEN!

HELPFUL POINTERS

- REMEMBER THERE IS SO MUCH MORE OUT THERE IN LIFE.
- MOTIVATE YOURSELF TO THINK AND ACT POSITIVELY.
- DO NOT WAIT FOR THINGS TO CHANGE, YOU HAVE TO MAKE THEM CHANGE.
- DISREGARD ANY NEGATIVE FEELINGS PEOPLE HAVE TOWARDS YOU.
- ACCEPT YOU HAVE A PROBLEM , THEN FIND THE SOLUTION.
- KEEP YOUR MIND OCCUPIED WITH POSITIVE THOUGHTS.

There is more than one job out there, more than one partner, more friends and much more in life still to be discovered, so go out there and make your life the happiest and best it can ever be.

CHAPTER 8

COMMUNICATION

It is one of the many ways we progress in our lives through the most basic of skills nature has given us, a gift which amazingly most people just seem to waste. The gift of communication, whether it is through speech, body language or any form of emotional skills we develop. The ability to communicate correctly will always be a great asset throughout our lives.

So why is it then that so many people lack the basics of good communication? Simple, lack of confidence, lack of thought. Now if you listen to a confident person speak, they have everyone around them in a hypnotic state, whether what they are saying is of interest or not. People are amazed and admire a person who has the confidence to communicate so eloquently with a relaxed and skilful manner.

You too can have this ability and confidence to communicate in a respected manner throughout your life. The key to good communication is to think first of what you need to say and also how best to say it.

Take a basic telephone call you are going to make about a business whose standard of service fell far short of your expectations. Many times I made the mistake of storming in there, all guns blazing, hurling masses of abuse down the telephone at the first person to answer, then feeling such a fool when all I did was vent my anger on the poor receptionist who was just doing her job by answering my call; then by the time I had got through to the person I needed to speak to my anger and frustration had simply dissipated as disappointment in myself had then materialised. I have in the past even done this in public, venting my anger as soon as I entered the premises.

NOT ANYMORE!

What I now realise is the best way to win an argument or complaint is maintain a very calm relaxed mature manner. In this way you will be treated with far more respect, also you will be able to think in a more constructive manner. The moment we become angry we lose all ability to think and act rationally. It is very difficult to function correctly when we allow our emotions to control us.

Through a telephone conversation or in person, maintain a very relaxed and calm approach. Now I know this may be difficult if someone has done you an injustice. Yes, you do sometimes feel like stoving their head in. We have all felt like that and look where the people who have adopted this method of solving a problem or dealing with confrontation have ended up. Yes, in prison or dead, now is that what you want?

Now when I need to make a telephone call to make a complaint, I write down exactly what I need to say at the time I feel very angry, then I do not make the call at that time and am always so grateful that I did not, because when I read back what I was going to say it was full of threats and abuse which would have gained me nothing.

Those who know me have described me as a very intelligent and relaxed guy with a very understanding and easygoing nature, who can also be very aggressive. It is this aggressiveness that allows me to progress successfully as a Stuntman, this aggressiveness I adopt in my working day is controlled and used to my advantage to perform to the best of my ability.

That is exactly how aggression should be used: in a constructive manner, not to harm or upset anyone. Unfortunately when we feel disappointed we become angry and thus our calm attitude changes for the worse; after our argument or displeasure with another person's mistake has vented, we then calm back down and after some thought, most of the time we feel very let down and let down with whom? OURSELVES. Yes, we sometimes take a step back and deeply regret our actions. We have all done it, said some very cruel and hurtful words or hit out and then once rational thinking has returned, yes, we regret it.

WE CANNOT TURN THE CLOCK BACK

If only we could. Face up to reality, we cannot, so if you are in the unfortunate situation of a blazing argument, be very careful what you say and do because that few seconds of anger can dramatically change the rest of your life very much for the worse. I know it is not easy. I have many times been involved in arguments or hit out at someone; sometimes yes, they deserved it, and sometimes what I said needed saying.

Now as a more mature person, I look back with regret and realise that there was a much better way of dealing with the situation than the attitude I adopted back then. In 2009 my then girlfriend was a nightmare, 'thick as pigshit' as I have stated, just 'tits & fanny', a 'Ferrari without an engine'. You could not reason with her, she was far too thick, no matter how wrong she was and she always was, she would not or could not admit it. On meeting her mother, I could see why: LEARNED BEHAVIOUR. Her mother was as thick as pigshit too.

Thick people are by far the worst people to have an argument with because they do not realise just how thick they are. My ex was stupid and lacked the social skills to conduct herself in day-to-day life, so in an argument that she had always caused she could not and would not back down and accept that she was wrong.

This taught me a life lesson, what I did not want in my life, and that she had to go.

WE LIVE AND LEARN

Yes, we do live and learn, as I have mentioned before and it is worth mentioning again; as long as we live, we will make mistakes and learn. The more successful you aspire to be, the more mistakes and knockbacks you will encounter. I lived and learned with many a girlfriend who I knew was not right for me: however, try telling my Big Dick that.

The choice is yours, you and I both know that in the time you have taken so far to read my work, you have in your own thoughts experienced some of the problems and traumas I have experienced; also you have become more confident in your thoughts and actions, as it is simply not possible to feel any negative effects from a book which is designed to help you better yourself.

Yes, my words are aggressive: for good reason, because I know what works, I have that life experience.

STOP BEING STUBBORN AND LISTEN

On many occasions I have listened to people giving others very good advice and have thought to myself just how right they were in their words. Be very careful that no one preys on your vulnerability to give you negative advice which will have a detrimental effect on both you and others. I have witnessed this happening so many times and more so today, with our shitty government wanting every boy, girl, child, insect going to university, to graduate three years later racked in debt with a degree not fit to wipe a tramp's ass with.

I see this every day: you could not make this shit up. Children, because that is all they are in their mind, going to university to get a degree in surf wave technology and the most common one which makes me piss myself every time, are you ready?

Media Studies, WHAT? I have worked for the past 31 years in the film and television industry, on over 700 productions, and never once have I met a single person who has a degree in Media Studies. I rest my case. Parents are encouraging Tabatha and Jeremy to build up debt, which they may never pay off, to eventually end up flipping burgers.

Now do not get me wrong, I am not against university. If your chosen career warrants going to university that is cool, some occupations do, however when I left school very few people went to university unless it was a necessary career progression. Our shitty government encouraged every child to go to university only to keep the unemployment figures down, they did not care about the volume of debt you were going to create, they even encouraged it with student loans.

So if Mummy and Daddy are pestering you, remember you ultimately have to be the one who makes the final decision and remember you have to also be the one to accept your actions and take responsibility. If I could turn back the clock, I would have left school at the age of eleven. I am self-educated and a genius, so what does that tell you about English education and, as I have stated, today teachers are just children themselves with no experience of life whatsoever, just thick children teaching children.

The relevance of good communication and confidence work as one; as you become more confident you become more relaxed and portray a greater intelligent manner which ultimately helps your communication. Remember, as I have said, communication is much more than the words we say, it is also our body language and the posture which we adopt which helps us to communicate.

Good communication, like the building of confidence, will take time. Be patient and work towards creating better communication and coupled with your ever-developing confidence the two will work together and always to your advantage.

THINK FIRST AND ACT LATER

As you have discovered I never thought about some of the aggressive words I chose in an argument or disagreement despite just how trivial the issue was. This, I now realise, was mainly down to bad communication skills and immaturity.

My lesson truly learned. Now I do think first and act later, much to my advantage, as being a confident person it can be all too easy to go firing in there, all guns blazing, and simply aim all your anger and aggression at the wrong person. So think first and think in a calm intelligent manner, remove all negative thoughts of violence and anti-social behaviour, because all you will do is lose massive respect and become ostracised. No one wants to be friends with a 'loose cannon', now, do they?

Unless your anger is directed towards the government! Remember, they are your enemy and you MUST be strong to deal with them and remember, they are The Shit on Your Shoes.

DO STAND UP FOR YOURSELF

It is no weakness to admit you were wrong or have made a mistake, far from it, because it takes a man to say he is sorry and admit he has made a mistake. Remember, we live and learn, and we learn from the many mistakes we make throughout our lives and believe me, I have made some whoppers.

It stuns me just how many people find it difficult to admit they messed up. I see it so much with my neighbour; he cannot accept that he is his own worst enemy. He cannot, no matter what happens, accept he made a mistake, he was wrong, he got it wrong, he did it wrong. He just does not have the social intelligence to accept he is shit at everything he does.

Again, this is the worst kind of person to deal with and be around. How can you progress if you are not willing to accept YOU made a mistake? Even rats know when they get things wrong. As I mentioned in a previous chapter, I had a friend who was only good at one thing: being shit! He was shite at everything: when he messed up it was down to the glue he was using, the temperature was too hot or too cold, it was never the fact that he did not know what the fuck he was doing.

I see this so much in life. You must be prepared to accept responsibility for your failings and also have the confidence and strength to call those out who do not. People who are incapable of accepting that they are the biggest fuck-up in life are deeply insecure. How do we learn? Through communication and by making mistakes, that is exactly how we progress. Do you really want those kinds of people working in bomb disposal?

It amazes me today just how shit most companies are at communication, and remember companies are run by people, relying too much on email rather than having a dedicated, manned by humans, telephone system. I believe this is purely down to the fact most people are so shite these days at speaking that the solution is to have everyone email everyone.

A previous friend of mine used to text me saying, "Are you home?" What exactly is that all about? I shall enlighten you. So because he did not have the social intelligence to make the telephone call and ask me the very question where he would have received the answer, he would choose to text me instead, a fine example of 'Shit4 Brainz'.

Communication

Never ask questions in a text message, never try to converse through text messaging: it will only lead to trouble.

I drive a considerable amount of time due to the nature of my work, so when my friend, shall we call him Richard? – let's do that, let's call him Richard – so I am driving and Richard sends me a text message asking me if I am home. I cannot look at that message until I have stopped my vehicle and turned my engine off. This is not going to happen until I am home, I am close to home less than 30 minutes away, so if Richard had the social intelligence to actually telephone me my vehicle would have allowed me through Bluetooth to speak to him and provide him with the answer. Now Richard was close to my home, was going to drop by, and instead of using his peanut of a brain he decided to text.

So when I arrived home some 30 minutes later, removed my ass from my car and read the text message awaiting me, I then proceeded to telephone him to give him my answer that I am now home. "Oh," Shit4Brainz replies, "I was close by yours and was going to drop by." Well if you had telephoned me like an adult you would have been able to wait some minutes for me to return home.

Text messages have their purpose but they are NOT a replacement for real speech. Ironically, I had to drop Richard from my life for a multitude of reasons. As you are very well aware I am ruthless and if you do not meet my very high standards and do not bring value to my life you are removed.

I am on-set and cannot have my cell phone with me because we are using pyrotechnic special effects and for the safety of cast and crew mobile communication is banned. I am doing a standard 10-hour day which may result in my additionally working three hours overtime, so if you do send me a text message you are not going to receive a reply until I am able. If you were to telephone me you could leave a voice message, your call will always be returned. So how come the simplest communication is lost?

Shall we just revert to smoke signals, drums or carrier pigeons? That is how messed up this world has become.

Some years ago, I tried to help a friend promote his automotive drawings. I have an excellent relationship with the team at both Ferrari and Lamborghini. I provided him with the contact telephone and email address of the key people. When I spoke to him to enquire how he was progressing this was the reply.

"I sent an email."

"You did, I presume this was after you had telephoned them?"

"No," he replied, he had not even bothered to communicate with them the correct way first. Ironically today he is working as a delivery driver.

No wonder today's generation is so messed up. Can you imagine if a war started, and the way the world is today it is a strong possibility that will happen, would we win? No chance, the current generation won't get themselves out of bed, they will be texting Sergeant Major to tell him they have a stomach ache.

If you could eventually prise their lazy fat ass onto the battlefield they would be texting the enemy, "Please don't shoot me, I have a Deliveroo on its way."

BE COOL

Good communication and confidence are about being relaxed and cool. Look at the people who stand out in life. It is the dark mysterious guy in the corner who has a relaxed posture and a confident look who will always grab your attention. In many employment interviews, it is the most relaxed, quietly spoken applicants who speak in a polite and respectful manner impress the most.

I do understand very well that it is not possible in this day and age to go through life not becoming angry with someone, as we are all different, we like different things and most importantly we all think differently. As I have said earlier in my writing, NOT EVERYONE IS LIKE YOU, and not everyone is like me. You may read my work and by the end of my book disagree with everything I have said.

THE CHOICE IS YOURS

That is simply your choice because I know what worked for me, what got me out of a back-street, very poorly paid job and motivated me into the great career I have now as a Stuntman, of which I enjoy every second and without confidence I would not be doing what I am doing today. To be successful you need self-belief. If you do not believe in yourself, how can you expect others to?

As my confidence developed, I noticed that my communication skills developed also. I no longer became the listener in a conversation. I now became an integral part of the conversation and was no longer just ignored. People desired to hear my views and experience and I welcomed this.

I will never allow anyone to grind me down to their level. If people think I am arrogant or big-headed for the way my confident attitude comes over then it is simply an issue they need to address, as I have worked hard and am proud of what I have achieved through being dedicated. Life can still be challenging. No one will ever get the better of me because for those who know me and know me well, I am a fighter, I survive whatever is thrown my way. As I said, "Nothing ruffles my feathers."

Entering into the world of stunts I had no idea just how shallow most of my colleagues were going to be towards me, not only shallow but also bitter, jealous and most of all insecure. What I was not prepared to do was allow them to control my success and control my future. As I have said previously and will continue to say, they are and always will be The Shit on My Shoes!

I have been through so much shit in my life, having to fight on the tough streets of Nottingham to survive, no way were these low life 'Shit4Brainz' losers going to control me.

I control me!

BE PREPARED

You too will experience some form of negativity; it is human nature. If you work hard and become successful people become jealous. Now we all know someone who suffers from jealousy, don't we?

Be strong. There are times when we all just feel like giving up. Sometimes even our best attempts to communicate with someone just fail. In these situations it can be best to step away, and let them deal with their own problem by themselves. If their problem then becomes your problem, and you need to communicate and through no fault of your own they fail to, this becomes very frustrating as you just feel you are being ignored and I know myself this only leads to frustration and anger.

In these frustrating situations take a big step back, relax and be as calm as possible to regain control. If you become angry, they do not suffer this anger, only you and those around you receive the brunt of your problem. Believe me from experience, if a problem is serious, they will eventually communicate with you. If it is a problem that you could easily let go of and move on from, then do so, for that becomes your best option.

I was able from a very young age to establish who are 'my kind of people', I do not need to surround myself with successful people to be successful. I do however like to surround myself with interesting people as communication is a fine art; I like to be able to surround myself with people who actually understand me.

HELPFUL POINTERS

- DO NOT ALLOW NEGATIVE EMOTIONS TO CONTROL YOUR MIND.
- A RELAXED CALM ATTITUDE WILL ALWAYS GIVE YOU THE LEADING EDGE.
- WE ALL ACT AND THINK DIFFERENTLY.
- HAVE MORE CONSIDERATION FOR OTHERS.

- GREAT COMMUNICATORS HAVE TO WORK HARD TO BECOME GREAT, AND STILL DO.

Like all things in life worth having, your confidence, communication, positive thinking and ultimately happiness will all take time to develop. They are all worth the many hours and years of effort you may have to dedicate to being the best communicator you possibly can be.

Do not ever lose the fine art of communication.

CHAPTER 9

DEVELOP A POSITIVE ATTITUDE TOWARDS YOUR LIFE

We have established that the most confident and positive of people do occasionally get down. Like our measure of fitness, the more confident and positive we are the better we become at dealing with negative situations. Through your reading of my work, you are beginning to realise that becoming more confident and positive is no big secret, your many thoughts, be they positive or negative, are the key to your development and success throughout your whole life.

SO HOW IS IT DONE?

Look at someone who possesses a certain skill, let's say a tightrope walker. No one is born with that skill already developed to perfection, but all the relevant factors to give one the ability are there. Firstly one must want to walk the tightrope, then be dedicated enough to partake in the many hours and years of training to build up the confidence and courage to perform the application.

DO YOU SEE WHERE I AM COMING FROM?

The key word is DEVELOP.

We all have to develop any skill to become better and work hard to master a particular project or occupation. We know it will not happen overnight, and once we realise this, we are much better prepared in our minds for the task ahead.

Over the years I have taught many people Kung-Fu, and each student has always made the association with dedication, time, fitness, and hard work. Once they realise just how difficult the art is to learn and once having witnessed a demonstration of Kung-Fu performed, they have also noted the relaxed and gracefulness of the practitioner. For many seconds of witnessed skill, many years of hard work and dedication have been endured to develop such expert ability.

As you have read, my confidence came from my partaking in Kung-Fu, as all martial arts are designed to develop strength, fitness, fighting skills, high moral values and most of all confidence.

You do not take your grading and having successfully passed be presented with a tablet which, once taken, instils confidence into your body. No, what you are presented with is a sash of a certain colour, depicting your achieved level, and a certificate. Not only do you take away visible achievements which can be displayed, you also walk away with a little more confidence in yourself than you first started with, as now you are DEVELOPING.

Now I am not suggesting that for you to develop confidence you will need to take up a martial art, far from it. Whatever you choose to do, choose it first because you enjoy it and, like all activities where you are mixing with people of different personalities, this will in itself help you to develop communication skills. These, coupled with your enjoyment of knowing the direction you choose to go in to better your future, will ensure that in time you will begin to see that you are closer to achieving greater confidence as time goes by.

Sadly, today people are not prepared for hard work, they are not prepared to fail, because our pathetic education system has them believing that 'we are all winners'. Well WE ARE NOT!

To prove it, take your life savings into a bookmaker's shop and put the fucker on the 3.30 at Kempton Park. Watch your chosen stallion fall at the first; now go and ask the bookmaker for your payout. Do let me know what happened. Despite the shit teachers today and our corrupt government are peddling, we are not all winners. You have to lose to DEVELOP. Look at losing as a positive.

Now I am a vegetarian, however, one has to admire KFC, Kentucky Fried

Chicken, and the Colonel Sanders story. A man who failed, lost, was broke, believed in himself, lost, broke, failed. The rest is history. Through failure we either give up or succeed, we give up or we find a way. Confident individuals are positive individuals, we always find a way.

Life is full of good and bad experiences, each and every experience you encounter will eventually have a positive effect upon your life, for once you manage to overcome any negative situation you will have added a little bit more confidence into your life provided you remain mentally strong within yourself.

Remember riding a bicycle, a skill you never forget. Can you remember the first time you rode without stabilisers? I remember that day very well, it was in Vernon Park in Basford, Nottingham, in 1972 when I was five. I fell, cut my knees and the palms of my hands, but I never gave up. It hurt, the cuts healed, I saw other children riding their bikes, a girl younger than me was riding without stabilisers; if she could do it, I could do it.

I was determined to succeed, I practised, I achieved. Today I have performed hundreds of bicycle stunts. I am one of the best Stuntmen in the world today because I endured.

I never give up!

WHAT IS CONFIDENCE?

Now this was the first chapter of my book so you have yourself some idea what confidence is and how it is represented. With all things in life, we never turn to self-help books until we need to. Like a first aid kit, we know it is there when we need it, we are more than grateful of its presence.

That is just what my book is for. IT IS YOUR FIRST AID BOOK.

Once you have acknowledged that you have a problem, then just like when you cut your finger and you do not allow yourself to unnecessarily bleed, you apply treatment. We know confidence is a state of mind, a belief in oneself and ability to be able to complete the most difficult of tasks, to be able to handle the most challenging of situations, calmly, positively and most of all successfully, to our own advantage. We develop confidence throughout our life's events and experiences, provided we adopt a positive frame of mind.

Your state of mind is the key to your happiness. As you have established throughout my writing, happiness is what we all aspire to. Having the ability to think in a positive manner will always lead you down the road to happiness.

In my employment as a cabinet maker, I worked with negative failures. In the 1980s when I occasionally saw a Ferrari on the road or a Lamborghini in a supercar showroom, I would aspire to achieve such rewards, so why did the friends who I was with view the same situation with a different reaction? Because they lacked confidence.

I would say, "One day I will have a Lamborghini, be famous, wealthy and successful." After my friends had finished pissing themselves laughing, they would say, "We don't have those chances, you will work in the gutter all your life just like we will." We will always be the losers in life. Did you note the word, WE?

I find this so much in life, people who are insecure always like to compare themselves to you.

You won't do it.

You won't win.

You will give up.

You will fail.

What they were actually saying is:

They won't do it.

They won't win.

They will give up.

They will fail.

A friend who is 5'6" once said to me, girls are not interested in short guys, they want tall guys. Now this may be true in some cases, there are women who prefer a tall guy, however the way my mind works is that there will also be women who will appreciate a decent guy no matter what his height. Now I am 5'3" and my fiancée is 6'3". Ironically my short friend is still single, enough said. Most of my girlfriends have been over 5'9" and with five-inch heels towered over me and I love it. Now that is confidence.

If their life is shit, they think your life is shit, if your life is not shit, they wish your life was shit. If your life is good, they don't want to believe your life is good. Remove them. They are toxic.

SO COME ON THEN HOW IS IT DONE?

This is a question so many people ask me. "How do you become confident, how do you think positively," especially when your world is falling apart around you.

I know from experience that it is very difficult to think positively when your world in your mind has just fallen apart. I have been there many times before and will unfortunately be there again in the future. It is THE NATURE OF THE BEAST. That is life. Life can and will at times be hard. Life at times will be cruel. Life at times will be shit.

Now you are understanding it: AT TIMES, not all the time, just at times. Remember what I said in previous chapters: IT IS ONLY TEMPORARY. Drive a car fast and hard constantly, you and it will eventually experience some form of problem. Keep the car in the garage and refuse to drive it. Problems will still arise. It is life, accept it, start disciplining your mind to think differently.

I had to do it. When I think back to my first job as a cabinet maker, I experienced bullying and verbal abuse on a daily basis. It was only with the confidence I developed through Kung-Fu that I was able to say,

"Enough is enough," and stand up for myself. I will never forget the shock on the face of my work colleague when I so aggressively turned. For him and all who witnessed the event the shock was so sudden and most of all surprising, that the total silence which fell upon the workshop just said it all.

My confidence was being developed and as time went on, and through my experience, I realised that by thinking in a positive way despite the many negative events that surrounded me, I always came out the winner. From that day on I was treated with far more respect and never did I suffer bullying or verbal abuse again. When I became a Stuntman certain colleagues were stupid enough to attempt to intimidate me, but this demonstrated just how thick they were.

They thought that because I was a probationary Stuntman and that I needed to dance to their tune that they could manipulate me. What they failed to understand was that I am Shaolin, I destroyed them. Bullying is rife in the film and television industry and the stunt section is by far the worst. I fight, what I was not prepared to do was allow 'The Shit on My Shoes' to control the direction my career was going to take.

When I entered the stunt world in 1993, I was not liked by a section of the stunt community. Why? Well you would have to ask them that question as 31 years later I still do not know. If I was to take a guess it is because I am powerful and they were scared of me. They saw my confidence as a threat and certain individuals tried to undermine me. They failed.

Are they driving around in an amazing Lamborghini?

Did they purchase three houses outright with cash?

Are they a millionaire?

I destroyed them. Many trainees become qualified probationary Stuntmen, succumb to bullying, crumble and lose. So why was I different? Why did I not crumble? It cost me £15,000 to train to become a

Stuntman; this was my money, not given to me to pay for my tuition, money I had earned, coupled with thousands of hours of hard work. To put it into perspective that is £36,000 today (2024).

Was I going to allow The Shit on My Shoes to win and destroy an amazing career? No way. I knew they were cowards: they were bullies. Stand up to a bully and you destroy them, they just dissolve away.

I was born and brought up on the tough streets of Nottingham, a Kung-Fu Expert and most of all CONFIDENT.

NO ONE CONTROLS ME!

I CONTROL ME!

YOU ARE IN CONTROL

So what you are now discovering is no secret. There are no secrets. If you want to become more confident you have to first change your mindset to think in a more positive and optimistic manner. I cannot come to your home and instil this confidence into you, it has to come from yourself. I can, however, help you, like I have helped many others become confident.

Through my life experience, I have bettered myself. Now no one made me take up Kung-Fu, this was my choice. You have already discovered that just making the telephone call to inquire about lessons was a massive milestone to cross in itself, let alone actually going to my first Kung-Fu class. The great fact is, I did it, yes, I did and this decision not only opened the door to my confidence it also led to my fascinating career as a Stuntman.

At times we all look to others for advice and sometimes we hope what we want to hear will be the motivation towards a better life. I still do discuss my thoughts and ideas with people whose opinions matter to me, but ultimately, I make the final decision. You are now aware that you need to develop a positive attitude towards your life to better yourself, to become confident, ultimately to be happy.

My chapters cover various stories, my life experience, friends, experiences both good and bad, and one thing I wish more than anything is that I had had this experience much earlier in life. However we all have to live with reality, life just is not like that and one of our many problems when we are younger is that our stubbornness becomes our own worst enemy. We want to go and find out for ourselves and that is exactly what we do, we find out the hard way, as many of us have discovered the hard way is exactly that, HARD.

It needed to be, as never will we ever forget a difficult upsetting incident or experience in our lives, and as I and many have said, "We live and learn," and as long as we learn then something good has come of a bad experience. What I was NOT prepared to do when I rewrote my book was be weak and write in a weak manner. The world has changed so much for the worse since I first started writing books in 2005. We have political correctness and diversity shit. A person should be chosen on one factor and one factor alone and that is merit.

We are at a point where our education system, police farce, judiciary, government are NOT fit for purpose. All riddled with failure and corruption. What chance have you got today if you are stupid and naive enough to actually believe the utter shit the government tells us; if you do, I cannot help you as you have already failed. My writing is to be appreciated and admired by individuals who want to succeed in life, those that yearn to be independent and successful.

As you are aware, I have disciplined my mind. I have several thought processes which constantly work for me; you could call them formulas, so let's do that, let's call them Riky's Formulas.

What Riky uses to keep his mind thinking and acting in a positive manner can be your survival techniques for life.

SO HAVE YOU REMEMBERED?

1) If it happens it happens.

2) It is only temporary.

3) We live and learn.

4) Easy to say, difficult to do, but not impossible.

5) Not everyone is like you.

6) Pick yourself up, dust yourself down and move on.

7) Please only one person, YOURSELF!

8) Current bad experiences are not necessarily what will be happening to you in your future.

9) Do not torture yourself with a problem, communicate with others to seek help.

10) Accept you have a problem.

11) A calm mind thinks logically.

12) Keep your mind occupied with positive thoughts.

13) Do not allow yourself to deteriorate.

14) Never give up.

15) Dissolve all negative thoughts.

16) Exercise.

17) Eat well.

18) Never neglect or abuse your health.

Most of all BELIEVE IN YOURSELF. As I have mentioned before, if you do not believe in yourself and your abilities, how can you expect anyone else to?

Occasionally things will not quite turn out as one would have liked. It happens, and the more you are able to accept this the better you will be at coping when these situations arise. We have covered 'mixing with the right kind of people' and as you are now fully aware, your chosen company will have a dramatic effect on your life both positively and negatively, and only when you have developed the strength to be a confident and positive person, to carve your own path and reject all negative communication that may come your way, will your life be a much better, healthier, rewarding and most of all happier one.

As you now realise, there is no secret to becoming confident and positive. You know that all the thoughts, good and bad, that enter into your mind are placed there by one person and one person only, YOU. So if you constantly think negatively, yes, bad things are sure to happen, and as you know, if you set out your stall to be a much happier one, guess what happens, yes you become a much happier and more positive person.

Even the most confident of people know that it is not possible to be 100% happy all of the time. However, which would you rather be? A confident, positive person who strives to be 100% happy or a negative person who sits around feeling sorry for themselves blaming everyone else for their misfortune, who is and always will be one of life's losers? Remember our M.O.D.E.L. citizen? This is just how our weak, pathetic and corrupt government want you to be, miserable, in debt, existing, not living.

THE CHOICE IS YOURS

As you have now realised, the way you will become confident and develop that positive attitude is in the key word, DEVELOP. You must have the discipline to be patient, qualities will only develop at your pace and the more you want to be the best person you can possibly be, the closer you are becoming each day to achieving your many goals.

I have many great achievements to date that I made happen throughout my life and there are many more I wish to accomplish. I will achieve everything in life I set out to do because so far, everything I have set out to do, I have had the confidence, courage and self-belief to achieve. One may say, well some of your expectations have not been realistic, for example, sitting with a group of friends telling them of my ambition to become a Stuntman and listening to all of their negative feedback and just thinking to myself, I will prove each and every one of you wrong – I did. When I became a Stuntman, some of them did apologise to me for doubting my ambition and drive. Anyone who knows Riky Ash will tell you he will never give up, he will always achieve exactly what he sets out to do.

He has developed a POSITIVE ATTITUDE TOWARDS LIFE.

You are now also aware that there is no magic formula to becoming confident, there is no secret, the only secret is right there in yourself. We are all capable of many great things, the only real obstacle that we place in our way is our own lack of confidence to see our goals and wishes through. The number one reason why the majority of people hold themselves back in every aspect of their life is because they are far too concerned about what other people think of them.

A conversation I had recently with a friend revealed just how unhappy he was and why he seemed to constantly feel this way. He found it very difficult to see any light at all, let alone a glimmer at the end of the tunnel. His reasons were as follows.

He was waiting for life to get better. Yes, he was waiting. Like you wait for a bus. Yes, the bus will eventually arrive, however what if you just walk up the road in the direction of the bus, it arrives much faster.

CREATE YOUR OWN HAPPINESS

If you are going to just sit there and wait for life to simply get better, you will be waiting a very long time, it just does not happen that way. You have to make it happen. You know this much as you have read it in previous chapters. If you want something to happen you have to make it happen, as nothing worth having comes to you that easily.

You now know from my writing that I concentrate only on the situations and people who make me happy and dismiss anything negative totally from my life. Cars make me happy. I love my Lamborghini, I love speed and love the freedom my supercar gives me, driving out with the roof down and even better when I am safely returning from a stunt job, driving my Lamborghini home with a great feeling of accomplishment.

SO WHAT ARE YOU WAITING FOR? Go out there and MAKE IT HAPPEN.

CHAPTER 10

ACHIEVING GOALS

When I look back at my many achievements and how I accomplished them, together with the many great achievements man has created throughout time, one element becomes apparent.

THE WILL TO SUCCEED.

The drive and ambition to be successful, the wish to invent, create or simply just better oneself for a more meaningful life. Whatever your reasons to be successful, and for all the reasons of the great inventors this world has ever seen, we all share one common fact.

IT IS WHAT WE WANTED

Remember when you were of an age when you just did not quite know what occupation to pursue, look at what employment you are now involved in. It is very rare to meet someone who is still doing the exact job they set out to do when leaving school. I myself left school at the age of 15 and became a cabinet maker, but by the age of 25 I was a Stuntman, a complete career transformation. At the time of leaving school more than anything I so wanted to work with wood, and I remember that on the day I secured my cabinet making job I was so happy. As time went by, I started to realise that even though I really enjoyed the work and the great satisfaction the job brought, despite having to work with people I simply did not like, this job, much as I enjoyed it, was so poorly paid that to have a better quality of life my employment situation had to change.

As our life progresses, we do realise that changes have to take place. Situations will dramatically change your life. You have to decide what is right for you. In your teenage years you can be forgiven for not knowing exactly what direction you would like your life to go in, but if you are in your forties and reading my work and still do not know what direction you want to take in your life then the hard truth is You Never Will.

YES IT IS CONTROVERSIAL

As I have stated in previous chapters, my writing is controversial for many a good reason, but remember this is a self-help book; it is designed and written for that exact reason, TO HELP YOU. It is not written to make you feel good, make you feel worthwhile, that is your job, not mine.

I worked down a backstreet in Netherfield, Nottingham, where I was referred to as a toerag. I still to this day have no idea what that meant, it could have been a compliment for all I knew. Miserable Nev would not even call my name, he would whistle, like you whistle for a dog, if he wanted to gain my attention.

It was not until I took up Kung-Fu in 1988 that I ignored him until he called me Richard. Did it bother me being called a toerag? No, why should it? I am above all of that. I knew that I could progress towards a much better and rewarding life, my colleagues could not. They did not have the aptitude to better themselves.

I am not saying they were as thick as pigshit, far from it; they had some aptitude to become cabinet makers, wood veneerers, wood machinists and upholsterers. What they did not possess was self-belief that they could make their life any better. They also did not believe I could improve my life and often made the statement that I would work for Thomas Pearson all my working life. I was there for six years. I knew that with my ambition, cabinet making was not going to pay the bills.

Through my writing I tell it to you straight, not the shitty way our government attempts to con us. When you visit your doctor he also tells it to you straight, you may not like what he is telling you, but it is his job to do exactly that, whether you like it or not. If he did not give you the cold hard facts, he would not be doing his job properly and you would not be receiving the help you require. So stop feeling sorry for yourself and always expecting people to be nice to you and constantly telling you what you want to hear, not what you need to hear.

With Confidence

A past friend from Kung-Fu reconnected with me after 25 years. His wife had stopped him doing Kung-Fu, stating in her words that "It was shit". He had recently suffered a heart attack and he was also clinically obese.

Now if his scrubber of a wife had allowed him to continue his Kung-Fu he would have been in good shape and not in poor health. It became apparent in the conversation that his ugly wife was also clinically obese and taking thirteen different tablets each day. What kind of a life is that? I remember when he started Kung-Fu in 1988: he was, let's say, podgy, fat, a fat bastard. He trained hard and I mean hard. My attendance was exemplary, his too, very rarely did he miss a class, he would stay after our lesson had finished to use the free half an hour we were given to continue training without tuition.

He put the time in, he saw results, he lost weight, shaped up and felt much better in himself, looked better too. He progressed through his Kung-Fu sashes and was very happy. Then he 'mixed with the wrong kind of person'. A person who was controlling and manipulative, his new girlfriend, who eventually became his ugly wife with her ugly life and made it clear that he was not allowed to practice Kung-Fu anymore.

Ironically in 1989 I met a girl and dated her for a time, and she also made it clear that I was not to ever do Kung-Fu anymore, as all my attention should have been focused on her; the only part of her that my attention was focused on were her tits. She said I had to choose between her and Kung-Fu. Cracking tits or not, Kung-Fu won.

Cracking tits are everywhere. I could get that anytime, no woman was going to dictate my future, unlike my Kung-Fu friend who allowed his life to go to shit. His doctor said he needed to lose weight, his waster wife needed some kind of operation, whatever it was, the doctor said he would not operate until she had lost several stone. Apparently she went ballistic and so did my friend. I said to him, "Why are you both overweight anyway?" "It's the government's fault," he said. Now we all know the government is shite and the only thing any government is any good at is being shite. However, it is not the government's fault, the supermarket's fault, the world's food manufacturers' fault. If you are fat, it is your fault.

I will not tolerate any shite from anyone regarding people being overweight, it is simply your choice how much you choose to eat and how little you wish to exercise. If you eat less and move more, you WILL lose weight. Overweight people are lazy, simple as.

If you really wanted to lose weight you would. Now I could be obese and not train, if I did it would be my own doing and my own fault, no one else's. So how come people want to always blame everyone else for their own fuck-ups in life? I train two hours five days a week; the only exceptions are if I am working or I am ill. I cannot train at work, however when I return to my hotel I will swim and use the gym.

I never make excuses, I DO IT!

Achieving goals, I have achieved every goal I set myself. You can too.

WOULD YOU LIKE TO BE SUCCESSFUL?

You need to make a plan. The most successful people in the world are organised, they have to be. I write a list every evening of what I would like to achieve the following day. I use a pen and paper. I have done this for many years, I am an avid list maker, I get results. I never forget anything, I have everything written down, and did you know that doing that improves your memory, not that my memory needs improving. I have a photographic memory and remember everything. I can remember as far back as being only a few months' old.

MAKE YOUR PLAN

I do not know exactly what you would like to achieve but one thing is certain, you will need to make a plan, and by doing this you will be in a much better situation to succeed. Whatever you decide to accomplish and whatever direction you would like to travel in life, there is one vital point you must remember. The key to all success is SELF-BELIEF. Without this you will not succeed. Regardless of what anyone thought of my decision to become a Stuntman, the quality I had, and still do to this day, is self-belief. Whatever happens in my life I simply do not believe I can fail, my mindset is so strong.

Once I decide I am going to achieve something, I first research my subject in depth so that I have given myself the leading edge; I then make my plan. Look at all eventualities, set a strong foundation from the beginning and this base will be your vital strength throughout. It is good to hear the opinions of others but just be warned.

WE ARE ALL DIFFERENT

How many times have you been in a situation where you just cannot decide what you would like to do, because you are not quite sure? You ask others' advice. Now remember they may not have to live with your chosen decision and the law of averages tells us the more people we ask the more confused and undecided we become, because not everyone will give you the same answer.

So be warned, when you decide to do something or make a dramatic life-changing decision not everyone will give you the answer you hoped to hear. The choice is simply yours. If you are still at a point where you just become very confused, as you cannot decide what you want or which direction you would like your life to go in, then you still do not have the confidence and conviction to be yourself. Continually relying on others' advice will only keep you undecided for much longer and you will always remain a sheep, not the shepherd.

Do not get me wrong, whenever I have a vision, I do like to run ideas past certain people. Those who, firstly, are of a level of intelligence where they reasonably understand what I would like to achieve. I removed the shit out of my life long ago and I have the memories of the 1980s when I was the only one in my circle of friends with ambition. If I ask a person today for advice, it is because they matter to me. I am strong and do not become influenced by negative attitudes and toxic behaviour. I just do not do negativity and nor should you.

I HAVE THE LAST LAUGH

As I sit and write my book in my beautiful home which I bought outright with my earnings from my stunt work, I think back to the friends who, when I announced my ambition to break into the film and television

Achieving Goals

industry, laughed themselves silly. Be prepared to get laughed at, that is life, just remember if your friends do adopt this attitude just how good a friend are they anyway?

If you adopt a very simple approach to people's negativity towards you, your success will come to you even sooner than you imagined. Treat any negativity from friends regarding your ambitions as FUEL FOR YOUR FIRE. You are aware of these words from previous chapters; they work. The more my friends laughed and mocked me, the harder I trained to prove them wrong. Are any of them driving a Lamborghini?

WHO'S LAUGHING NOW?

You now know that you need a plan as your solid foundation for your future. You know you have to have self-belief. You may not like what you are about to read, but it is very important that you are made aware of it.

SACRIFICES

The more ambitious your goal, the greater the sacrifices become. It is not possible when you decide to work hard to achieve success that your current lifestyle will continue. If your goals are not too great, then you may not have to make any sacrifices to your lifestyle at all. However, if you aspire to greater things, the moment you decide to dedicate yourself to chase your dream your whole life will change dramatically. Are you ready and prepared for this?

How fast and far you are prepared to run is totally your decision. When I decided I wanted to be the very best I could be at Kung-Fu I attended every possible class and outside of the school environment I trained every day and even went to the trouble of creating a training area in my cabinet making workshop so I could train there too. Since taking up Kung-Fu in 1988 I constantly train even to this day. My hard work and dedication paid off; as you are aware, this dedication has led me into this most amazing occupation I have today. So yes, the choice is yours, you decide exactly what you wish to achieve, make your plan, do your research and next, THE APPLICATION.

DEDICATION

No way will your skills come to you without very hard work. Even if your ambition is not sport- or work-related and you simply would like to, let's say, shape up and become more healthy or give up smoking, the same applies, you make your plan, you do your research and then you apply yourself.

No one is going to do the exercises for you, and even if they did, you would not benefit. As I mentioned earlier on in my book, most people are lazy and will always stay that way. When you decide to set a goal for yourself that is exactly what it becomes, SOMETHING FOR YOU. No one is going to do all the hard work for you. You are going to be the one who will have to prise your ass out of your warm bed on a cold winter's morning to go out training. I had to do it many times myself and travel to Derbyshire for my hang-gliding lessons towards my stunt register qualifications, as well as work at my local stables to gain free riding lessons.

As I have stated people are overweight for two reasons; one, they consume far too much and two, they do not move enough. Eat less + move more = losing weight.

There are no secrets. How many miracle diets have we been subjected to over the years and people actually fall for this shit. Back in 2006 I dated a girl who wanted to lose weight. She was a nightmare, always checking the calories on food boxes, working out how much she could consume in a day. At no point did the lazy bitch do any exercise. I created her a training programme and offered to take her on walks to build up her stamina so that she could eventually run. Everything I suggested was met with a negative and direct anger towards me. We went our separate ways, and I was told last year that she is now a very unhappy 25 stone and it is everyone else's fault.

Nothing worth having in this life comes easily; if you have to work hard to achieve something, believe me, it is well worth having. If you are of an age where your parents are helping you motivate yourself towards your goal then this is good and do respect them for this, as they do not want to see

Achieving Goals

you end up down an alleyway with a needle sticking out of your arm.
You may feel sometimes you are being pushed in a direction you do not feel you want to go in and this is the point where you need to be strong and have a good look at where others are making you go, rather than in the direction you would freely choose. If you feel you are being channelled away from your true goals, and your happiness is being controlled by your parents, it is now time to let them know in the most diplomatic way, ENOUGH IS ENOUGH.

If you are reading this book and you are only 10 years old then I would say your parents are just doing their rightful job. If you are in your adult years and your parents still have a domineering control of you then words need to be spoken, and spoken right now.

My father, if you could call him that, was a very violent and controlling man. He wanted me to do what he wanted, by that I mean he wanted me to work in his fabric business. I had no interest in his business and as you know wanted to be a cabinet maker, as from the age of 10 I enjoyed working with wood, was very creative and practical. This did not have any impact on him, he became controlling and angry because I did not want to, as they say, follow in his footsteps. Let's talk about his footsteps, shall we? Built up a business, it failed, tried again, failed, house repossessed, burdened with debt, divorced from my mum, now he has a shitty life and a shitty wife.

I have developed the Midas Touch, whatever I invest in turns to gold, whatever he invests in turns to shit. Now one would think that with my wealth and success he would be begging for help and advice and want to know my strategy: no way, far too arrogant and jealous.

When I became a Stuntman in 1993, I had £7 in my current account and £3000 in a TESSA, a tax-efficient savings account which was later changed to an Individual Savings Account, a £300 van and a bag of woodworking tools. I am now a millionaire through hard work. No one helped me, no one funded me, I did it all by myself and I am very proud of that as so many people wrongly wrote me off.

It was through confidence that I was able to traverse down my chosen road and not live a miserable life working at my dad's factory. I stood up to him and he did not like it, who would? I did not care, I was going to do what I wanted to do, he was insignificant. As you are now aware, being confident and having this ability allows you so much more expression and freedom to just be yourself, and ultimately it is better to just be yourself than live your whole life in someone else's shadow.

BE PREPARED

The road to success, as you will discover, is riddled with potholes and hidden dangers. Believe me, it is no smooth road. For many years I have travelled this road and encountered various knockbacks along the way. I learned at a very early stage to be prepared for many more to come, because the more ambitious you are, the more susceptible you become to these encounters. Dealing with them is a different matter. Firstly look back at what the cause was, then learn from this mistake or creative criticism and just dust yourself down and carry on. You will become much tougher the more knockbacks you experience, up to a point where, like me, you become immune to any negativity.

It is not how many punches you can throw in life that will determine your strength: it is how many you are able to take.

Remember my words in previous chapters: Turn a Negative Experience into a Positive One and A Disciplined Mind. You cannot ruffle my feathers, I cannot be offended. No matter what abuse you hurl at me it will never have a negative effect on me, my mindset is that well-conditioned that I am not affected by any negativity towards me. Yes, NOTHING RUFFLES MY FEATHERS, NEVER HAS AND NEVER WILL.

Remember, diamonds are formed under extreme pressure: Be A Diamond.

You too can develop this confidence by reading, absorbing and then applying my work to your day-to-day life. Why would you allow others to affect you?

Many conversations I have had with friends have led them to a complete lifestyle change, be it giving up smoking or deciding to get into shape or something as easy as just saying no to a dominant family member who just keeps asking far too much of them. They look at my life and want to be Riky Ash, because I have what everyone wants: confidence. What I have is also achievable by every human being. Not everyone will become a millionaire, not everyone will be an inventor or establish a successful business, but anyone can become confident, so why do people choose not to? Because they are too concerned with what other people will think of them, they are too scared to shine, just in case someone dislikes them. As you are aware, I judge my success not by how many people actually like me, but by how many people actually dislike me, because I know if people dislike me I am doing things right.

COMMUNICATION IS THE KEY

We can acquire so much knowledge from each other if only we have the confidence to communicate. I ask lots of questions, I like to converse, I am interested, I want to find out, I like to know and by adopting this attitude, I discover, and remember you can never have enough knowledge. Chat to people, dedicate some of your time to establish how they became who they are today and how they achieved success, what drove them, how they coped with knockbacks and how satisfied they are with what they have achieved.

If you want to know, ASK. If you do not ask, you do not get, simple as that. We can all learn something positive from each other.

When I decided I wanted to become a Stuntman, I made contact with various established Stuntmen, arranged to meet with them and asked for their help and advice, as they were the very people who were doing exactly what I was training to do. I also enrolled in drama school, and this became a valuable asset to aid my stunt career, as to date I have had several major acting roles in various television programmes, television commercials and feature films, all of which I am very proud of.

In 1983 I was working with a joiner in Hucknall, Nottingham, the famous

With Confidence

resting place of John Byron. I was on what was called a Youth Training Scheme, set up by the government to provide you with a job for one year with a weekly salary of £25 per week, equivalent of £105 today. Ironically that was the very figure I was earning in 1990 when I left my cabinet making job at Thomas Pearson.

We had a tradesman by the name of Denis, who worked at Hucknall colliery as a bricklayer. On his days off he would do work on the side for cash for my boss. We were putting a new roof onto a terraced house when Denis asked me what time the owner brought the tea and biscuits out. I informed him that we had not received any. "You have been here how long and no tea? Fuck that." He called the boss, Richard, over. "Where is the tea and biscuits?" Richard's answer was that the customer had not made us any. Denis was not having any of this. "Richard," he said, referring to me, "Go and knock hard on the door and ask what time he is making the tea and don't forget the biscuits." Now I was only 16 and had never done anything like that before, so I was hesitant. Denis asked me was I cold, did I not want a drink and a plate of biscuits, and he then said something that has resonated with me to this very day: IF YOU DON'T ASK YOU DON'T GET. I have never forgotten those very words and they are so true. If you don't ask you don't get.

I knocked on the customer's door, saying Denis on the roof would like to know what time he was making the tea and don't forget the biscuits. Really when you think about it, we should not have needed to ask, anyone with any manners would automatically do this.

If I want something I ask, I am not shy. I ask for help if I need help, I will ask to borrow if I need something, I ask for information all the time.

I ask, I get!

Whatever direction you aspire to go in, you need to have a very positive strong mind, as your encounters with physical and mental obstacles will be sometimes unexpectedly frequent. You need to continue forward with strength, as if those obstructions are simply not there. This, as you are now aware, can be done by always adopting a positive attitude.

You are now starting to see the relevance of having a disciplined mind. There will be times when others will give you that motivation you may require just to get you back on the road to success and once you have dusted yourself down and continued with your goal you will find it becomes much easier to be that little bit stronger.

YOU WILL TOUGHEN UP

As we know, life is hard at times; it is just the way it is and unfortunately the way it always will be. No one will ever be able to change the traumatic events we sometimes experience throughout life. As you have discovered you do become tougher as time goes by and this toughness becomes a great asset to our future life.

I have accepted that because of my chosen career I will always have to dedicate a considerable amount of time to training to keep myself in the best shape I can be, and also to have all the relevant skills required to do my job correctly and safely. I am used to constant training from Kung-Fu and this dedication to training was adapted to accommodate the many hours required to keep my stunt skills current.

Unfortunately, because of the nature of my work I have suffered injuries and was told by a very experienced Stuntman that sooner or later, if you are working on a regular basis, you will succumb to injury. I accept it is part of my work and sometimes it will happen and if I keep myself as fit, supple and as strong as I possibly can, I will be in the best possible position to aid a speedy recovery and get myself back to peak physical fitness.

The same can be said of experiencing knockbacks. If you aspire to give up smoking or lose weight, yes it will be hard at first, however as time passes it will become easier. Remember you are not the first person to have encountered these problems. You have two choices in anything you choose to do, CONTINUE OR QUIT. I did say it was simple, and what could be more simple than those two words. Now I know what you are thinking, It is much easier to quit than continue, so how does one overcome quitting by wanting to continue?

POWER

Power from the strongest part of your body, YOUR MIND. We all at times suffer from some form of weakness, this is perfectly normal. Controlling that weakness is another thing. Sometimes our wish to better ourselves, be it through health, employment or education, is not solely for our own benefit. I have had many conversations with people who have suffered heart attacks; it was only when their thoughts of not ever seeing their children growing up changed their mindset instantly for the better, encouraging them to lead a healthier lifestyle. It is a shame that someone has to experience trauma to realise that. Now I do not know what has happened in your life so far that has encouraged you to read my book. It has become apparent to you just how relevant that each and every chapter is to becoming confident.

Look at each chapter as being a part of a very interesting jigsaw puzzle. You can pick up any piece of that puzzle at any time; once you remember how relevant that piece is to your life you can, when you need to, pick up another piece and so on until in your mind you feel very confident of your future self and ability. As much as you need to keep yourself physically fit, you also need to condition your mind.

My early life was shit, my current life could have been shit; I could have just stagnated and watched everyone else having so much enjoyment, that would have been easy. It would have been easy to stay miserable and have a shit life. I did not want that kind of life, Shit Life, Shit Wife, living in Shitsville. I took action, I Made It Happen. I worked on my mind, my mindset, my visualisation of how I wanted my life to look. I read millionaire mindset books and when everyone else was listening to music I was listening to motivational and success cassette tapes. I would purposely visit Graypaul Ferrari's dealership in Loughborough at the age of 19 and look at the cars. I would drive past millionaire mansions and watch documentaries about successful people. I was fascinated by success.

I became physically and mentally stronger. Yes, I would encounter negativity; the people who were being negative towards me were simply, The Shit on My Shoes. That is exactly how I had conditioned my mind.

HELPFUL POINTERS

- DECIDE EXACTLY WHAT YOU WOULD LIKE TO ACHIEVE.
- MAKE YOUR PLAN.
- BE PREPARED FOR KNOCKBACKS.
- KEEP YOURSELF IN THE BEST OF HEALTH.
- EXPECT TO HAVE TO MAKE SACRIFICES.
- TOUGHEN UP.
- VISUALISE SUCCESS.
- NEVER GIVE UP.

Whatever direction you wish your life to progress in, never neglect your health and never allow anyone to manipulate you along your hard road to success, no matter how disrespectful, heartless or cruel they are towards you, because THEY SIMPLY DO NOT MATTER.

YOU, YOUR FAMILY AND YOUR VERY CLOSE FRIENDS ARE TRULY THE ONLY ONES WHO REALLY MATTER.

CHAPTER 11

BECOME MORE ASSERTIVE WITHIN YOURSELF

Many people have a great ability to tell others what to do or give out very helpful advice, but when it comes to their own life they fall far short of their own expectations. The sayers in life, NOT the doers.

As you have read in previous chapters, becoming a more confident person will take considerable time to achieve: however one sure thing, it is possible and achievable, only if you can become more assertive within yourself and are prepared to WORK HARD.

You can read many self-help books and listen to hour upon hour of advice; however, all is wasted if you are not able to put it all into practice. There are far too many phrases such as I will do it tomorrow, I will do it on my day off, I will do it at the weekend. You have to stop saying I will and get on and do it. If something needs to be done, no amount of words will get the job or application achieved; you have to be prepared to get off your sorry ass and do it.

What you have realised is that it is only as difficult or as easy as you make it. You also know that both positive and negative thoughts within your mind are placed and kept there by you, and you only. As you are also aware, you now know the value of disregarding all negative thoughts and replacing those with more positive and constructive ones that will help and enhance your life.

Any time I desire to better myself, be it through health, work or for other constructive reasons, I assert an authority over my mindset and examine my aims and ambitions. Through discipline and dedication, I set my mind to focus and work hard to achieve exactly what I set out to do. I make all my goals achievable, despite how outrageous and ambitious others would perceive them to be. Over the years I have realised that if you are confident in yourself, you will succeed. If you attack a project with dedication you will, in time, ultimately succeed, if you have any doubts within yourself whatsoever, you will fail.

Take the example of someone trying to lose weight. I myself being of the correct weight for my height and build, one would say how would I know what it was like to try and lose excess fat? Well, I have been there too. Back in 1985 I participated in powerlifting and went from being nine stones up to eleven stones in weight. Now because I was training very hard, being this weight was by no means damaging to my health. I was still very fit and able to run many miles, but when I started to train in Kung-Fu, weighing eleven stones proved to be a great problem for my build.

Kung-Fu requires amazing amounts of strength, coupled with fitness, both of which I had. Something very important in all dynamic physical activity is suppleness, which was something I massively lacked and the only way to become more supple was through regular training and through the loss of excess weight, so that is exactly what I had to do.

BECOME A DOER NOT A SAYER

How many times have you promised yourself and others you are going to do something to improve both your and your family's lives for the better? You say what you intend to do and maybe you acquire all the information and the equipment to do it, then BANG, you fill your mind with all negative reasons for not pursuing your goal, well you refer to them as reasons, but really they are just excuses for you lacking confidence in yourself and your abilities to carry your ambitions and wishes forward.

Many people decide to address the problem of being overweight and when asked why they are that way, they mostly reply, "Because I eat too much." Very rarely do you ever hear them say, "Because I do not exercise," or they will tell you shit like it's my thyroid, it's my genes, never I Am Lazy!

When I realised that I needed to lose two stones to be the correct weight for my Kung-Fu to develop, I decided to address this immediately by designing a training programme which I strictly followed and which worked for me. Within four months I was down to nine stone, looked and felt noticeably better and to this date, have maintained that weight and constantly improved on my fitness. Because I am dedicated. I am a doer, NOT a sayer. You do not even need a gym.

There are many examples of people who have dedicated themselves and have lost masses of weight and look like a completely different person, and have managed to maintain that healthy shape and all credit to them, because it is not easy. They did it and so can you.

Be it losing weight, giving up smoking, drinking or something completely out of the ordinary you would like to achieve, you can if you truly want to and are prepared to suffer the hard work and masses of effort it will take. It is going to hurt. Becoming more assertive within yourself your mindset will think in a more constructive way. As I have said, there are an awful lot of sayers out there in life and very few doers.

It is quite true that the more you experience a situation, the more confident you become in the future with similar situations. I get asked on a regular basis, "How do you become more confident?", "How do you become positive?", "How can I be more assertive?" The answer is simple.

Firstly, as you very well know, you need to want to, and secondly, it is through PRACTICE.

Someone once said to me, "Well you make it sound so easy."

Yes we are all different and all our circumstances and reasons in life do differ, however we all aspire to be HAPPY. Or much happier than we may be at this present time.

You have read about SNAKES AND LADDERS, you also know that we are all riding the ROLLER COASTER OF LIFE. You also know that how fast and far you run in life is simply your decision.

I have made many sacrifices throughout my life to become the best person I possibly can be and still will dedicate my time to the things I truly enjoy which make my life better and much happier. Yes, there are times in my life when I have to be more assertive with myself. In past relationships I have been very thoughtful and easy going and unfortunately women have taken full advantage of this and used it against me. So I learned a great lesson from my experience, that if you are really kind and generous to someone they will unfortunately take full advantage of this and use you. Those shitty girlfriends, the Users, Losers and Fakes, I removed from my life. They will always be nothing, insignificant because they did not have the social intelligence to be successful in their own right, their intention was to leech off my success. They are and always will be, nobodies going nowhere fast!

It is simply true, as you hear many people say, "I need to toughen up, as I just get used," and it is so true. If you allow someone to manipulate you, they will take full advantage of your kindness and unfortunately you will be the one who becomes hurt, as I full well know.

When you read 'Welcome to The Real World' you will be reading the real truth about what life is really all about and what life is really like. As I have said, this book is written to help you, so you will be reading JUST WHAT YOU NEED TO HEAR, NOT WHAT YOU WANT TO HEAR.

That is the benefit of my book. By now you will have established that I do speak my mind and what I say simply is the truth, and it works. I do not do Political Correctness shite. I tell it just as it is. I WILL NOT BE SILENCED.

You will never succeed in life if you are weak.

From now on, only say to yourself what you truly will dedicate yourself to achieve and not what you would like to achieve. You know your reason for reading my book is to become a confident and happy person and one thing is for sure, my words resonate.

PIECES OF THE PUZZLE

If you look back over each chapter you will see, if you have not already realised it, that each chapter complements the others. When you first realised that you lacked confidence and went looking for help, you would have established that any acquired learning process is broken down into segments which makes the information much easier to absorb.

Even though my book is structured this way you could choose any chapter at random and read it at any point in your life and it will always be relevant. Look at each chapter as a piece of a puzzle you are trying to construct. In reality, whatever chapter you decide to read at any point will only have positive results towards making you much happier and more confident within yourself.

A SHARP TOOL IN A SKILFUL HAND

If you have a strong foundation, reasonable skills, knowledge, dedication and a will to succeed, then that is exactly what you will do. You will succeed, you will progress and will become a much better person with a more rewarding life. To progress throughout our life, to become positive and confident we do need, coupled with life experiences both good and bad, some tools to help us. Be it through good advice or a self-help book like the one you are reading now, these tools will always be of great use to help you achieve your chosen goal.

Use these acquired skills positively and constructively and you and others will see just how fast and far you have managed to run, and you are still not out of breath.

When I left school, as you are aware I became a cabinet maker and loved the job very much, but not the people I worked with. Looking back, many great things came of becoming a cabinet maker and possessing the woodworking skills I now have for the rest of my life. The same is true of becoming more confident. I now have these skills for the duration of my life, and it is so true, YOU NEVER FORGET HOW TO RIDE A BICYCLE.

When you have read my book, do read it over and over again, and you will notice that throughout time you do not need to read it as often, as firstly you start to notice yourself becoming more confident and secondly you start to remember just what the book said. As you apply this to your life and to any future problems you may have, like all things in life, PRACTICE MAKES AS PERFECT, AS ONE POSSIBLY CAN BE.

EXPERIENCE IS THE KEY

As you are very well aware whatever your occupation in life, or hobbies and interests, as time passes provided you dedicate a degree of time to your chosen subject you do progress. The same can be said of your becoming more confident. If you attended a job interview every day for one month, I am sure that as time went by you would become more relaxed and comfortable with the whole interview process. You would look back and say to yourself, "I just wish I possessed that confidence at the first interview." As you can see quite clearly, EXPERIENCE IS THE KEY.

If you regularly work out you see positive results, work hard you see positive results, keep training you see positive results, no one who puts the time and effort in and works hard doesn't see results.

As an active Stuntman, I have progressed to excellence at my job throughout the years and have been very fortunate to work on a regular basis, so the many skills needed to be a safe and skilful Stuntman continually become more honed and perfected as time goes by.

This is no different for you in becoming more confident. Just think back to your first ever job interview, your first driving lesson or even your first date; remember how nervous you were and now look back to how you are today in those very situations. Through constant exposure to certain situations, we become much better able to cope, THE FEAR OF THE UNKNOWN soon dissipates.

Many people would find it a very daunting experience having to stand up in front of a very large group of people and conduct a talk. I am regularly booked as an after dinner speaker to talk about my work as a Stuntman and have developed my skills through the many opportunities I have been presented with to be a great speaker. This has never unnerved me as throughout my working day I perform in front of many people, so am not fazed in any way by people watching me. I am now The Strategist, I mentor business people, I help people create great wealth, I am a problem solver and I get paid handsomely for having those skills. Skills that I alone have developed.

I can tell you that when people become nervous about having to present themselves in front of a crowd, it would not matter if there were one or one hundred people present, they would still be as nervous. The only way of possibly eliminating this fear is to conquer it, and the same can be said of any phobia. You can live and suffer it and allow it to control you or you can be assertive within yourself and say, ENOUGH IS ENOUGH and attack your problem face on. The more we associate ourselves with situations we deem to be difficult, the easier they become. Remember as I have mentioned earlier – it is a very important factor in your becoming confident – we are all different. What scares you will not scare me. I am fearless.

CHALLENGE YOUR FEARS

We have established that by reading my work you would like to become more confident within yourself. As you know from reading previous chapters there is no big secret to becoming confident, as you will also realise, any phobia you have can and will be encountered only if you are prepared to challenge that phobia face-on and assert authority over yourself and your mindset.

Running away from these problems only delays your actions to square up and face them. You have to learn to acclimatise around your fears. Experience is the key. The more exposure you have, be it being afraid of the dark or heights, gradually build yourself slowly into these situations and you will start to become more comfortable within your surroundings to a point when you yourself will look back and wonder what all the fuss was about. It is referred to in the stunt world as acclimatisation.

YOU ARE HOLDING YOURSELF BACK

The only person who is preventing you from being a more positive and confident person is you. It is human nature to sometimes be afraid, we all experience the occasional adrenaline rush, some more than others. When you allow your fears to control you, that is exactly what they do, they control you, they prevent you from leading a much more creative, fulfilling and happier life.

I myself encountered difficulty with water right up until I was 24. When I decided I wanted to be a Stuntman the thought that entered my mind was water and my lack of skill with it. I was not frightened of water, but the problem was I could barely swim very far and not for very long. Now if I had been asked to do a drowning scene as a Stuntman, I can assure you that with my limited ability in water it would have been a convincing one.

I did not want to carry with me into a new career my difficulty in water so I decided to do something about it. One of the qualifications of the many required to become a Stuntman was swimming, so I decided I would choose that as one of my qualifications towards my training.

When I enquired about lessons the swimming instructor was fully aware of adults of all ages not being able to swim correctly or at all. Through regular lessons I was able to develop my swimming to the required stunt register standard by constantly exposing myself to it. Regular acclimatisation made each lesson more and more comfortable and enjoyable. I even swam in rivers to expose myself to a more realistic environment for stunt work, to also experience cold water shock. I even swam at night. So to this day I no longer have that discomfort of water and have safely performed many dangerous stunts for television and film successfully with this skill.

In 1988 when I started Kung-Fu my instructor told the assembled class that there was an opportunity for two students, grades of orange sash or above, to go to Hanover, Germany, all expenses paid for one week to fight in the German Open. So who would like to go? I was hesitant to put up my hand even though I knew I was good enough; my hesitation cost me and taught me a valuable lesson. Two other students beat me to it and off they flew to Germany for the time of their life. When they returned to the school they were treated as heroes, photographs of their experience were placed upon the noticeboard and their trophies put on display, everyone wanted to know them and learn any new techniques they had acquired. The students who received the all-expenses-paid experience were no better than me, they just had the confidence to say, "I am good enough." I hesitated and missed out. The following year the same opportunity arose, only this time before my Kung-Fu instructor had finished what he was saying, not only was my hand up but I shouted, "I am good enough," and off I went with another student to Hanover.

Today I never say, I am good enough; I say, I AM THE BEST!

THE HARDEST OF ROCK CAN BE PENETRATED BY A SINGLE DROP OF WATER

Every experience you encounter in your life, either good or bad, will have a positive effect on your mind. Once you have set your mind, created your plan and begun to dedicate yourself to your chosen goal, you will start to realise that through regular dedication your dreams are not too far out of reach.

Even something as gentle as a drop of water dripping constantly onto granite will eventually wear the hard rock away, and that is exactly what you will do. Each time you experience a difficult situation or a life-changing decision, you will slowly but surely develop a little more confidence as the days go on, which will help to enhance your mind to solve any problems with comfort and ease and will also eliminate stress, because now, as a confident person, you will think in a more logical manner and take all information, both positive and negative, on board, eliminate all irrelevant information and only concentrate on what really matters to help you find the solution that works best for you.

As time passes by, you will start to develop more confidence. New situations will gradually become easier to cope with. Just as I mentioned earlier, the more exposure you experience the more immune you become to the situation.

So next time when you discipline someone or give advice, look at your own life as it stands and ask yourself, am I becoming more assertive within myself? Am I now starting to become more disciplined and doing exactly what I keep telling myself I would like to do?

Or am I just one of the many sayers in life?

HELPFUL POINTERS

- STOP DOUBTING YOURSELF.
- START WORKING ON BEING HAPPY.
- BE STRONG WITHIN YOURSELF.
- ACCEPT THERE WILL BE TIMES WHEN YOU WILL FEEL WEAK.
- EXPERIENCE WILL HELP YOU BECOME STRONGER.
- YOU TAKE CONTROL OF YOUR LIFE.
- STOP SAYING AND START DOING.

Whatever you aspire to, it is there for the taking, so go out there and get it, just like I did when I said, "I am good enough." Be strong. If at any point you feel yourself slipping back into your old ways do read this chapter and other chapters over and over again until you find you no longer need to read about what you should be doing, because you will be doing just what you want to be doing. Progressing to become a more constructive and positive person with your thoughts and beliefs.

Be assertive!

CHAPTER 12

WELCOME TO THE REAL WORLD

I first wrote this book in 2005. It is now 2024. What prompted me to rewrite it was that so much has changed in the past 19 years and sadly not for the better. The world has gone to shit, England, as my friend Roger rightfully put it, is totally fucked. It is now a shithole governed by utter corruption, our judicial system is broken, our police are now referred to as a police farce, they are inadequate and our MPs are pathetic, only taking on the role for their own gratification (the only exception being Nigel Farage who has just been elected to parliament I am delighted to report, and who is going to completely change the appalling reputation that MPs carry). Most MPs are as thick as pigshit with no common sense whatsoever. Our education system is worthless, young people today are being failed.

The media and entertainment industry I work in is run by 'wokeism' and diversity has messed everything up. A person should be employed on one value and one value only and that is MERIT. Can they actually do the job? That today is no longer a consideration so an employer can put a tick in the diversity box. You have to be both physically and mentally strong to survive today otherwise you will be destroyed.

Regardless of just how confident you have become since starting to read my book there are some very important facts you must know, some of which will be apparent and some not so.

Sometimes we have a habit of kidding ourselves and sheltering from the truth. One thing I made sure of before I began to write my book was not to fall into the nicely nicely trap that many self-help books tend to do. As I have mentioned earlier in my book, I will tell you what you need to hear, not what you want to hear, and that is more apparent today than ever before. Our shitty government wants you to be their slave, accumulate debt and be dependent until you finally die broke.

Facefuck and Twatter did not even exist when I first typed my words and the internet was in its infancy, and we still have a parasitical monarchy which should have been abolished long ago.

Confident people change the world for the better, they stand up to injustice, stand up to our corrupt government; we only have to look at the Post Office scandal to establish just how ruthless our government actually is. From the age of 19 I was able to work all of this out, just how controlling our government is and times were much better back in 1987.

Looking today at 2024 I am so pleased I have the confidence to be me, to be strong and write in my unconventional way. I have succeeded in life because I chose to be different, a leader not a follower. Most people are existing and not living.

Being confident will not change other people's thoughts and feelings, they have to change themselves and also want to change. As you are aware, I used to become very frustrated by unreliable people constantly letting me down, turning up late, failing to arrive and never returning my calls. I am sure you too know someone or several people who are just like this, SELFISH, self-centred and always thinking of themselves and showing no consideration for others.

Now if you have read this far and also absorbed the information contained within the pages of my work you too will know exactly how to deal with such people and handle future situations. If you have read this far and are saying to yourself, no, I do not know how, then you need to get back to the beginning of this book and this time concentrate and absorb the information. I have established through my life's experiences, that most people are totally unreliable, forgetful, selfish, thoughtless and lazy. They do not care about me, and they sure do not care about you.

What you now have to start to do is move well away from being bothered by other people's ways; as you know, neither you nor I can change the way people behave. As you have read in previous chapters, they have to first want to change the way they are, then begin the change, and sadly most people are far too lazy to do that.

FOR EVERY NEGATIVE THERE IS A POSITIVE

The simple way I deal with people with an unreliable selfish and downright thoughtless nature is that they will never amount to anything, which for someone who is positive and confident becomes a good thing because I then have much less competition and so do you. Your will to be successful and be the best person you possibly can be only makes your dreams and ambitions much easier to achieve as the negative GOING NOWHERE FAST thoughtless, unreliable and lazy amongst us will not have that drive and true fighting spirit to better themselves to achieve, making it a clear road for those who do aspire to be more confident and lead a much more fulfilling life.

Remember these unreliable people do not matter and if you have to unfortunately have dealings with such people in your day-to-day life, as we all sometimes do, just take a step back and think of this.

As you are now very well aware not everyone is like you. Not everyone shares your feelings, thoughts and beliefs. Not everyone thinks like you do and not everyone will agree with you. So stop right now and look at what you have already achieved in your life and what you plan to achieve in the future.

Delete from your mind right now other people's attitudes and bad manners. Make it your problem and it becomes a problem, and a problem you can well do without. Once you realise that no two people are the same you will be in a much better state of mind to deal with people who fall far short of your expectations. As you have read, if you expect others to do as you do, unfortunately it is you who becomes disappointed. Is it really worth getting yourself into such a state over another insignificant person's thoughts or opinions?

Just be polite and move on. You will never progress if you continually drag yourself down worrying about people who simply never have and never will matter. If you would like to be a confident person and have a happy successful lifestyle, just remember these very important words that you read in Chapter 10.

IN LIFE IT IS NOT THE AMOUNT OF PUNCHES YOU CAN THROW, IT IS THE AMOUNT YOU ARE ABLE TO CONSTANTLY TAKE THAT WILL MAKE YOU CONFIDENT AND SUCCESSFUL.

Now you get out there and stop feeling sorry for yourself and if you think that life has dealt you an unfair hand then get off your ass and do something about it, just like I and many other people had to. We have made our life much more happier and fulfilling by *hard work* and *self-belief*, so there is nothing preventing you from doing exactly the same.

STOP KIDDING YOURSELF

Very few people really do care. Simple as that, it is the truth. Do not go throughout your life believing that people really do care about you. Yes, your close family hopefully do, however as we know in some extreme cases they do not. Some families will kill each other over a pound note. They may rip each other off, constantly lie and cheat each other. Friends can sometimes be exactly the same.

When my confidence developed to the level it is at today, I quickly realised that I now became the minority, and you will too. You will now stand out from the crowd, be the one who most people will turn to for advice and BE PREPARED because it is a true fact that people will attach themselves to you like a leech to become more confident and then when they think they do not need you anymore they will drop you like a stone in a pond. That is life, that is how most people are, so get used to it because believe me it will come your way, like it has come my way many times before and will continue to come my way many times in the future, only now I am wise, I can psychoanalyse absolutely anyone.

YOU WILL GET USED

Yes it will happen, people prefer being around a confident person, one thing most people who lack confidence hate is being told what to do, regardless of their lives being a total mess and completely out of control. They come to you for help, you sit them down and give them the real advice they need OR DO YOU? Do you tell them what they really need to know or do you tell them what they want to hear? Well if you come to me for advice and your life has gone to the shitter one thing is for certain you would probably go away hating me because I will have told you what you needed to hear not what you wanted to hear.

Anyone who knows me will tell you I do not mince my words. I will tell it to you honestly and straight. I will hit you with it square on in the face, I will tell you exactly what you are doing wrong and what you now need to start doing correctly to make your life travel in a positive direction. Sometimes unfortunately people retaliate with, "And I thought you were my friend," while they are crying into their cornflakes. Well wake up, that is why I am telling you straight, because I am your friend and if you want to get yourself out of the shithole you are in right now I suggest you listen.

Remember it is not my problem. I can happily walk away if it does not affect me, but be prepared as I have said, people will always take positive advice on board. Unfortunately when they do get themselves back onto the straight and narrow, they have long forgotten who really helped them to get there.

I HAVE BEEN THERE TOO

I do not want to dwell on my past behaviour and past negative experiences. Let's just say, YOU LIVE AND LEARN. Unfortunately I learned the hard way. You may be reading this and saying to yourself, who does he think he is telling me to get my house in order? Well I will not tell you who I am, just you find out for yourself, because I am not that very poorly paid backstreet cabinet maker struggling to survive that I used to be. I am a real person just like you, and a very successful one at that, who is now a millionaire.

BE INSPIRED.

In my late teenage years, I did not get in with the wrong crowd, I was the wrong crowd. If you got on the wrong side of me you knew about it and knew about it fast. I did not mince my words back then and I sure did not make idle threats, and I did not go looking for trouble but if it came my way it became very bad news for the recipient.

Now we do tend to associate bad behaviour with individuals of low intelligence; however I am sure you will have established that I am not of low intelligence. I sure have more intelligence now than I did back then. Yes I got into trouble, I did a lot of bad things. Am I proud of what I did? No. Do I regret what I did? No, and the reason being, because what I did back then has made me the kind-hearted, considerate, caring gentleman people describe me as today.

We all do make mistakes, and we always will. As long as we are able to learn a positive lesson from our mistakes and admit we were wrong we are making good progress in the right direction. That is one of the many reasons I hate MPs and our corrupt government because they are answerable to no one, they constantly lie and cheat and go unpunished, they set by far the worst example to our generation. They are and until things change for the positive, the shit on my shoes.

They want you to fail, they do not want you to be independent, have courage and strength, they need you to be subservient and obey their every command.

Fuck them!

The only politician I have anytime and respect for is Nigel Farage, now that is a Man of Confidence.

Nobody controls me, I control me! I have created my own set of rules for life, I do not obey our corrupt antiquated laws, I have created my own set of laws for my life.

I ONLY HAVE TO JUSTIFY MY ACTIONS TO MYSELF.

YOU THINK YOU KNOW

Well, you may be shocked to realise that you do not know everyone, and you sure do not know what others are thinking. Being a confident person will make you more alert and somewhat more observant, however one sure thing, it does not matter just how confident you are, you just truly do not know everyone.

I was conned and taken for a ride by a girlfriend who one would only say just how sweet a girl she was. No way would I have ever thought that she would stoop so low and turn out to be a fake. She constantly led me on with what I now know to be several lies which not only shocked me but also really upset me that someone so close to me could con everyone around her into believing she was such a nice girl. Her true colours eventually shone through and both my friends and family were as disgusted as I was when her shallow nature finally surfaced. We shall refer to her as Bitch Features.

Well for me that was another lesson learned, not everyone is what they seem, and not everyone is what they make themselves out to be. So beware, as I have so rightfully said, most people do not care who they hurt throughout their lives and will constantly lie and be dishonest until the day the guilt finally sets in and believe me it always does. So you remember what you have read in previous chapters, THEY DO NOT MATTER. They were your past, their cruel ways will eventually backfire on them and they get exposed as a fake.

NOBODY'S FOOL

Now as you have realised, by your own thoughts you can control your life to create more happiness and success for yourself and for those who really matter in your life. Do not waste your valuable time and newly earned confidence on no-hopers and wasters, the negative individuals of this world.

As I have stated, THEY DO NOT MATTER and as time passes by, you soon realise, if you have not already done so, that these people should be avoided at all costs and kept well out of your life. Have another read of MIXING WITH THE RIGHT KIND OF PEOPLE and you will see exactly what I mean.

Unfortunately, because of your confident persona people will try and take you for a fool. They will try and leech confidence out of you, try to use you and falsely become your friend. Now it is totally down to you to stand firm and prevent yourself from being used. By all means do help those genuine people out there who are sincere, however do always be on your guard for the users of this world who will constantly TAKE TAKE TAKE; when finished you will not see their fat lazy ass for dust and you will be the one sitting there looking like a fool.

THE TRUTH SURE HURTS

Now for my own reasons I am an atheist. When I was allowed to have my own freedom of choice I happily and so gladly dropped religion without one thought of regret. Now I am not going to tell you what to do regarding your own religious beliefs, I do not need to because you are now becoming a more confident and positive person who is now enjoying a much happier and rewarding life. So you decide your own views on religion.

I would like to share with you my feelings on the subject of control.

Religion is CONTROL.

Government is CONTROL.

I control my life NOT religion and certainly NOT our corrupt government.

I was born and brought up a Roman Catholic, due to my mother's beliefs. My mother still to this day is a practising Roman Catholic, but I am a Roman Catholic no longer since 1997. So what changed my mind? It was simply one person, me. Over the years of being religious, I had regularly attended Sunday Mass, received my Confirmation as all Roman Catholics do. I even attended weekly Mass. Was I a good Roman Catholic? Yes and no. Was I a good person would be a more valid question. Yes, I could be good and I sure could be bad if I had good reason to be. Throughout my childhood I was terrified of God, I was a strong believer that whatever I thought, or negative action I had undertaken God would know and if it was bad, I would be punished.

I lived my life in a very unhappy way, always thinking, will this upset God?

So throughout my childhood I missed out on so many activities as I thought God would not approve and would punish me harshly. I was so embroiled in religion that I carried relics in my wallet, Jesus Christ took pride of place on my bedroom wall, and in every vehicle I owned Saint Christopher, who we were raised to believe was the patron saint of travellers, sat on my dashboard keeping me safe.

When I reached seventeen, I was a wild teenager, involving myself in a gang, partaking in violent fights with regular vandalism and unsocial behaviour thrown in. My way of justifying what I did was to attend confession on a Friday evening so that all my evil sins could be forgiven then carry out the same or sometimes even worse behaviour the following week.

Religion is hypocritical, there is one word and one word only that sums up all religions and that word is, CONTROL!

Religion has been created by man to control man, to make man think that there is a higher being referred to as God who will judge the way you have conducted your life on earth and make the decision whether your final resting place will be Heaven or Hell or that you will be reincarnated back on earth as a slug.

IN LIFE YOU MAKE YOUR OWN HEAVEN AND YOUR OWN HELL.

I too was foolish enough to fall into this control trap. Religion has been designed to control you as a person and control the way you think and act.

Religion has caused more wars, devastation and loss of life throughout this world for thousands of years. "If you do not believe in what we believe in, we will kill you." Not very Godly, is it now? Now reading this you may yourself be very religious and believe in God, that is simply your own choice. I have chosen to be an atheist and I am very proud of the fact and that is my choice.

Now some people reach out to their religion to carry them, I do not need to do that, I carry myself. Some people reach out to their religion for strength, I do not need to do that as I have the ability to provide myself with strength.

I do not rely on witchcraft, religion, old wives' tales, to control my life, I control my life!

So what made me decide in January 1997 that I was going to become an atheist and proud? I was sick of my mind being brainwashed and controlled. I had simply seen enough of life to establish that God has been created by man, not the other way around.

Man created God to control man, to keep man in check. Religion is very powerful if you are weak-minded as anyone who believes in religion is. Religion is there simply to keep control of you. To some it dictates who one marries, it dictates where one lives, what amount of one's income they decide to give to their said religion.

I too was foolish enough as a teenager who earned very little to toss coins into a collection basket when I could not even afford the bus fare to get myself to work. So in 1997 I decided my life and the way I thought it was going to change in my favour, I was no longer going to be controlled. If I decided to do something I was never again going to think, will this offend God?

I now established that God was fabricated by man so we can be controlled. I applied this way of thinking also to the law of the land, which again is there for one purpose and one purpose only, to control us. How immensely liberating 1997 became. From that day forward I did not have to justify my actions. I could conduct myself just how I pleased and decided upon my own law of life.

The law of my life works very well for me. It is to this very law that I attribute my continued success. I simply do what I like, lawful or unlawful. The government does not control me, I control me!

Most people walk this earth allowing religion to suppress their life; I do not allow anything to suppress my life. Yes, I do succumb to illness just like any other human being, but what I refuse to do is believe that this illness was a punishment from God. When I have a problem in life I do not hit the floor on my knees, hands clasped in prayer, asking a person that does not even exist for the answer; I resolve the problem with my own strength of mind and character.

You may disagree with everything I have written, you may have your own agenda, you may agree, what is vitally important is that it does not matter what you think. For I have the strength to decide, which is exactly what I have done. I destroyed all my religious relics, removed all evidence of religion from my life and made it known to my family and friends that I was a Roman Catholic no longer, now becoming an atheist and proud!

It is fascinating how so called intelligent human beings have throughout time fabricated this very strange belief system for their own gain.

When travelling back from collecting a new car in Germany I stayed in the Belgium city of Ghent. Ghent has three magnificent cathedrals, apparently funded by the stupidity of human beings who were led to believe that the money that they donated to the church would secure them a closer place to God.

So foolish as some human beings can be, many residents of Ghent donated vast amounts of their wealth to the Church to secure one of the best seats in the house, not having the common sense and social intelligence to realise that when one passes away, one either rots in the ground, gets burnt or is thrown into the sea.

I feel as we progress as human beings that we will eventually leave this primitive way of thinking behind and have a completely atheist world, a much better world at that as one man will not feel the need to stove the head in of the next man in the name of God and religion.

Now where religion is concerned, I was sick of being dictated to and told that this or that was a sin. I do not want to live my life in regret and worry that I may have upset God. Now when I see all of the troubles throughout the world and people willing to kill each other in the name of religion I am proud of myself for being able to say that I am no part of this brainwashed pathetic fucked-up behaviour.

I made my decision in my life not to be controlled by something I do not believe exists. I do not follow any form of religion, and I sure do not believe in God.

God is like PVC, man-made.

I lead my own life and have an envied confidence for being able to just be myself and be so proud of who I am.

Now as I have mentioned, the choice is totally yours. You make your own mind up over this one. As I have stated so rightly before, do not allow anyone else to create your path, you create it by yourself, and you decide just what direction you would like to travel in.

I have the strength and confidence to believe in myself and so can you. I do not suffer a weakness where I have to believe in something that simply does not exist. I do not need a religion to carry me, I carry myself, I do not need a religion to give me strength, I already have strength. I do not need a religion to give me vision, I already have vision. I sure do not need a religion to tell me what I can and cannot do.

I ONLY HAVE TO JUSTIFY MY ACTIONS TO MYSELF.

NEVER HIDE AWAY FROM YOUR PROBLEMS

Only a cowardly fool hides away from problems in life. If you choose to adopt this shallow approach when faced with a problem then I shall tell you exactly where you will end up. Much worse off than you were before you so foolishly buried your head in the sand hoping that when you decided to appear all your problems would have disappeared by themselves and guess what, they did not. Now you are looking an even greater fool than you were before you decided to run away.

All you do when you adopt this pathetic attitude is prolong the problem and make it worse, which also can lead to anger and resentment for those around you that may also be affected by your cowardly approach.

Problems never have and never will go away on their own and this is another fine reason I so rightly rejected religion because I do not believe kneeling down and talking to an imaginary friend. I believe that 'God will help me and only God can help me now' attitude is just a sign of a lack of confidence and weakness in oneself. Face up to your problems yourself. Have the confidence and intelligence to understand that unless you address your problems face-on as they happen you will never endure.

Back in 2007 an associate of mine was struggling financially, all brought on by his inadequacy to stabilise and run a prosperous business. He had no business acumen whatsoever, was talentless and would have been better off working at Wickes.

The only thing he was good at was being shit. He would keep throwing good money after bad, keep borrowing more and more money, instead of accepting that he was never going to be a businessman. Some people have it, some people do not, that is life. What he did was hide away from his problems, those very problems that he had created to the point of going bankrupt, he lost what little he had. He was far too stubborn to listen to an expert like me, a person who had built several successful businesses from absolutely nothing. In my book *From Mini To Millionaire* I tell you how I did it.

Never back away from your problems, everything, no matter what, can be solved.

SUFFER THIS NO LONGER

For some time now you have been reading my work. You have dedicated many hours to cultivating yourself into a confident and positive person. One thing that can never be denied is that this book can and will only bring you positive results if you are prepared to dedicate the time and energy into being the most confident person you possibly can be.

Never hide yourself away from the real world and never build a barrier around yourself and live your life like it is a fucking fairy tale. It is not a fairy tale. Yes, you may be sorry to be told, this can be a cruel heartless world we live in. Get used to it because it is not going to change. Just because we live in such an imperfect world does not allow you good reason to join the many evil people out there who so much enjoy the unnecessary hardship and hurt they so regularly inflict upon others.

A colleague of mine had, for many years, suffered from stress, which had unfortunately resulted in him suffering a heart attack. During our conversation he now realised that his constant worrying, inability to relax and just be himself had been brought on by him getting his life all stressed out because he found it very difficult to understand why other people were not like him; and this conflicting mindset became detrimental to his health.

Now as you have earlier read, NOT EVERYONE IS LIKE YOU, so is it worth getting all stressed out over something you simply cannot change? Do not allow yourself to fall into the trap of wanting to change the world. Yes the world is currently a right shithole brought on by corruption, pathetic religion and greed.

The reality is most people are unreliable, as I have stated; very few people have the common decency to return your calls unless they want something from you to work in their favour; then they act as though you are their best friend. If you ask someone to do something for you most people either forget or make such a mess of it and get it wrong that it results in you having to do it yourself anyway. Then there are those who lie to you that they have done what you asked of them. Unfortunately we have all experienced someone like that.

As long as you allow yourself to suffer these kinds of people, they will inevitably always control you. Now as you are becoming more confident within yourself you will begin to realise you are no longer suffering these types of people any more than necessary. Confidence To Be You. Confidence To Say NO.

Each time you pick up my book and read any part of it you become that little bit stronger, just like you are building bricks into your wall. You will start to become more thoughtful towards others, and disregard all your so-called friends. Just remember this; now you tell me how good is your friend if your friendship resides on a one-way street? By that I mean, if it is always you who has to constantly make the phone calls and always pay them a visit and yet they never telephone or visit you?

Remember what is written above, SUFFER THIS NO LONGER. Now do just this from now on: make that phone call to your so-called friends, you know, the ones who are unreliable and never contact you. After telephoning, write the date down when you called them and do not phone them again. See just how long it takes for them to call you and if six months passes and you have not received any form of communication then they are your friend no longer, write them off as they are not worth knowing.

Also never be fobbed off with the excuse 'Sorry I was so busy'. No one is that busy that they do not have 30 seconds to dial a friend's number. Get yourself into the understanding of 'the real world' and you will always be on the winning side.

If you allow yourself to become worked up because someone never phoned when they said they would then all you will ever do is drag yourself down. You know my feelings on WORRY, it is unnecessary and only leads to poor health. As long as you are in the WORRY STATE OF MIND you will never allow yourself to progress towards being a much happier and healthier person.

WHAT HONESTY?

Do not kid yourself any further that most people are honest, as they are not. How many times have you been let down or lied to by people, because most people will always please themselves, without any regard for your feelings. The ongoing problem of honesty and the lack of it is unfortunately a colossal issue as we are governed by very dishonest people; this in turn leads to resentment and further dishonesty.

Many times I have heard people say, why should they be honest when we have such a dishonest power force? Our Police Farce, courts, governments, local councils are all dishonest, because that kind of employment attracts dishonest self-serving people. I read lots of books, not shitty novels or sci-fi, I read proper books, books that inspire and educate me, that provide me with knowledge and understanding.

How do you think most of the high-profile criminals in this country manage to hide their crimes? They have to have corrupt police officers working for them. It has happened many times before and it will keep happening, it works on the 'need and greed' principle and the fact that the reward is far greater than the punishment.

Sadly there are very few positive role models left in the world today. Need And Greed has taken control. All MPs are liars. Today we have 650 members of parliament, yes, 650 useless fuckers all gathered together to totally fuck up our country and they do a very good job of it. When you finally confront a liar, they sometimes can be too spineless to admit their weakness and fault and continually lie to you, which only makes matters much worse.

Just be very careful who you trust and remember:

A MAN WHO TRUSTS NO ONE IS A MAN TO BE TRUSTED

I do not trust anyone; I can be trusted.

Confidence allows me to speak my mind. So many people lack the confidence to be powerful and strong.

When journalists ask questions of members of the public in the street, you hear so many comments such as "I am not sure", "I don't know", "They might be". Journalists either seek out the 'Shit4Brainz' of society or most people are too afraid to speak their mind, in case they may offend someone. Which one are you?

You were born to shine, so start shining. Be courageous to stand out.

Being confident will make you more honest with yourself and those around you because you will feel at ease being yourself and speaking your mind. Now I always speak my mind and as you are very well aware I am proud to have the confidence to be this way, as I would not be comfortable with myself if I adopted a more dishonest approach.

If you ask me, I will tell you what I think. I will tell it to you straight and this world would be a much better place if we all adopted this attitude. It is important to hear the truth. It is no good encouraging someone into a career if they lack the aptitude it takes to progress and be successful, otherwise they will become very resentful and disillusioned with those who they feel betrayed them.

Have the confidence to be honest towards people; if they are shit at something and you tell them so and they take offence, then they are just substantiating your words. Just learn to be honest and if they take offence to your helping them then move on, as no matter how hard you try you will never be able to help a person who cannot take constructive criticism. Remember what you have read earlier in this chapter. It is not how much you can give, it is how much you can take, that really matters.

Some people will never learn.

If someone chooses to be lazy and it affects you, remove them from your life if possible. I truly hate lazy people.

HOW MUCH DOES IT REALLY COST?

I can tell you it costs you nothing to be polite and have good manners. Now we should all possess this necessary social skill and if you are reading this and lack the basics of politeness and good manners I suggest you go tell whoever dragged you up that they have failed, because our ability to have these skills stems from our parenting.

You have no excuse for being bad-mannered. Would you like it if someone was bad-mannered towards you, never said please or thank you? How would you feel, if you helped someone and they never bothered to thank you?

So if it costs so little, why is it then that some people lack these simplest of skills. It stems back to what I have stated earlier, SELFISH, THOUGHTLESS AND DOWNRIGHT UNGRATEFUL.

As I have stated, YOU WILL NEVER CHANGE THEM, they have to change themselves and want to change. Do not let them ruffle your feathers, do as little as possible for these people and if they do not show you respect and good manners, pull them up on the subject immediately.

NEVER BE AFRAID TO SPEAK YOUR MIND

If you are not prepared to stand up for yourself, you will get used. If someone's behaviour is having a negative effect on your life and you allow this to continue, the individual involved will continue causing you constant distress, as it is human nature for certain people of low intelligence and lack of consideration for others to continue in this way, until you have the courage to face them and put the situation well under your control.

You and the people around you will notice many positive changes in your persona from becoming more confident. As you are now aware, when my confidence developed both my friends, family and work colleagues noticed the change. For I no longer lacked the confidence which was holding me back from just doing exactly what I wanted to do and from also just wanting to be myself.

Some people may find your becoming more confident a threat, and will become frightened of you as they no longer feel they have the power and control over you that they once held. See this as a good step forward for yourself in the right direction as your life should be controlled by you and not by others who have no right over your mind and future.

You will make enemies; it is the nature of the beast. Do not be afraid of this and do not ever let it bother you enough for it to result in worry and stress. I have many people who hate me, does it bother me? No, why should it, the more you hate me the more I know I am doing the right thing as sadly we live in a world of envy and jealousy where certain individuals do not want to see people succeed, they want you to fail, and if you do fail they take great pleasure in it.

Look at successful businessmen and the way they brush off criticism from their competitors; they just keep fighting on, no matter what is thrown in their direction and this is exactly what you must do too. I regularly receive negativity from my colleagues in the stunt world and it does not and will never bother me as it is simply not possible to become successful at something without encountering some form of jealousy and resentment.

As you are now aware, if people choose not to like you, because you have the confidence to be yourself and speak your mind, then that is simply a problem they need to address, not you. Just leave them to it, look at what you have so far achieved and just look at what they have not and you will see just like I do why you and I are on the winning side and they are not and never will be.

You too can have the ability to always speak your mind as you now hopefully will have the added confidence to carry you forward in a more positive manner.

In time you will have courage to just be yourself and be able to have the strength to make important decisions without having to rely on other people's negative views and opinions, which, as you are well aware, can sometimes lead to stress and confusion as our differences can cause a person who lacks confidence some confusion.

YOU ARE NEARLY THERE

It has taken some time to read my work and yes you have nearly completed my book. you may place my book down with many thoughts running through your head, both positive and negative. However, I am sure when I say this, that the positive thoughts are diluting away all the negative thoughts you may have had, as you know there is always a way, and you are finding your way right now.

Remember you may not agree with anything I say, you may agree with some or all of it, that is purely your right to choose, just as I have chosen my path in life.

Sit back for a few seconds and just think of all the positive things you are going to now achieve in your life, focus on that confidence.
Remember:

CONFIDENCE IS A STATE OF MIND.

CHAPTER 13

CREATING YOUR OWN HAPPINESS

By the time you reach this section of my book you may not be aware that I have had to have my original book With Confidence republished. The reason is that my original publisher let me down and let me down in a big way. Now as you are aware I was new to the world of publishing and a new author, I had never written more than a story at school or written work for my Kung-Fu theory exams, so entering the big wide world of publishing was a completely new experience, an experience that has educated me.

Sometimes in life bad or negative experiences can leave us in good stead for future experiences one may encounter. Just because things do not work out for us the first time around, that does not mean that every time we try something new it will go wrong or fail. My publisher could have been fantastic but unfortunately they were not; the same can be said about people, if everyone adopted a caring nature instead of being selfish as most people unfortunately are we would live in a much happier healthier world.

When things do go wrong in your life do not do as most people do and expect every car, relationship, job, project or whatever to fail.

IF YOU THINK FAIL YOU WILL FAIL

You need to wake up and wake up fast if you are the kind of person who labels everyone the same. We are all different. NOT EVERYONE IS LIKE YOU, as I have said many times throughout my book and I will keep saying it, because it is a very important point.

I had a recent conversation with a friend who had for the past three years experienced very bad relationships with men. The men she dated showed a pint of beer more attention than her. She endured their selfish behaviour, hoping they would change and unfortunately until they had drunk the last drop of alcohol in the land they would never change.

Unfortunately, my friend is frightened to fall in love. She has now met a new man, one who is very hardworking, respectable and honest, and who shows her lots of love and affection and who is devoted to her. She tells me she has not put much effort into her new relationship because she is frightened to have her heart broken again. Well if this is how she or anyone feels about the world of relationships DO NOT DATE it is as simple as that. I know of couples who have been together for 25 years or more who have unfortunately broken up.

Relationships are by far the most complex part of life; you have two people with different personalities, different temperaments, different thoughts, who come together and the only way a relationship will work is if both parties put maximum effort into it. Be understanding towards each other's needs, thoughtful and loving, true and faithful and guys, be a good listener.

If one partner keeps putting effort in and the other does not and shows a selfish nature, then the other person will only be able to endure so much. We all have feelings, and what is the point of being with someone who does not enhance your life and make you happy?

So if you are entering a new relationship do not and never judge your new partner by your old. Yes, there are some very cruel heartless people out there, I know, as unfortunately I dated one and I am sure many of you have too. Remember, a bad experience does not mean that in your life that is all you will experience. Keep throwing the darts at the board and your will eventually hit a bullseye. It is called the law of averages. You have two choices, you can either give up and never progress and never succeed, or you can with HARD WORK and dedication keep trying. You will be amazed at what you can and will achieve.

As I have always said, if two people want to be together, they will do anything to be together. If you are in a relationship where you keep making all the effort, but your partner would rather put more energy into seeing their friends than seeing you, then you know just how much you mean to them. It will make you feel like second best, make you feel unwanted. What you have to ask yourself is, how long are you prepared to endure such selfish behaviour? Look at it this way: if the person really wanted to be with you they would make maximum effort to be with you, it would hurt them when they were not with you and they would be counting down the days until they could be with you again.

Whatever you decide, and I do hope it will be to be together and work things out, please do remember everyone has feelings and DO NOT ever neglect your partner because you may think because you are young, handsome or attractive that you have the world at your feet and plenty of time for dating. A stern warning, you can spend the rest of your life trying to replace true love once you have lost it, and many people never do.

FIND ANOTHER WAY

My mindset works as follows.

If something does not quite work out for me, I will find another way. I will look for other options, I will research, I will look for other avenues, I will just keep going until I find what works for me. I adopt this in every aspect of my life. If I am looking for a new car, something for my home, an item of equipment for my occupation, I never rush into any decisions without giving it plenty of thought and without researching all my options.

You can adopt this attitude towards your life; why should you be rushed into making a decision that you may well regret? I always say that if you and only you make the decision then if all does not quite work out as planned then you have only yourself to blame.

COMPLAIN, COMPLAIN, COMPLAIN

Never be afraid to complain. It is your right if you experienced bad service, be it a product you have purchased, a service you have paid for or whatever it may be, if you feel that your rights have been infringed never be afraid to complain, no matter how trivial the situation may be.

Creating your own Happiness

The standard of service today is shite, customer service has been replaced by chat bots, major companies are wondering why they are going into receivership, they need me managing them. Every company should have a contact number so those of us with the social intelligence to actually be able to use a telephone can call them.

I hate complaining; however it is something that I am having to do more and more as we seem to now live in a world where people just do not value their customers anymore. An example of a very bad experience I had resulted in a court victory against Mercedes-Benz. I like to say that I wiped the floor with them. My experience proves that it is always worthwhile to complain. My bad experience with Mercedes-Benz happened when purchasing a new car for my business; the opportunity arose for me to collect my purchase from the factory in Germany.

Now one would think that a company like Mercedes-Benz could get this right. No, the whole experience was riddled with problems throughout, from the flight, airport pickups, the hotel, and even at the Mercedes-Benz collection centre. This very poor standard of service from Mercedes-Benz led me to write several letters of complaint. I even wrote one to the company director of Mercedes-Benz, and what kind of reply did I receive? A simple 'yes, we admit we made mistakes and got things wrong but we at Mercedes-Benz do not offer compensation'. Utter bollox. As my friend Roger rightfully said, "Arrogant Bastards."

When reading those words it was like a red rag to a bull, it angered me so much that I had just purchased a new car, and that Mercedes-Benz messed up and messed up bigtime, then they had the arrogance to say, "We at Mercedes-Benz do not offer compensation." Every reply I received from Mercedes-Benz carried words of arrogance, and shithole excuses, nothing solid and nothing to make me feel valued as a customer. I was not going to let Mercedes-Benz get away with treating me like this, offering me shoddy service and attempting to fob me off with pathetic excuses. I did what I thought was right and took Mercedes-Benz to court and won.

It was so satisfying to stand up in court and defend myself and wipe the floor with them. I just thought, is that the best you can do Mercedes-Benz? I was very pleased to hear, in the judge's summing up, his words, "Mercedes-Benz are not the motor company they used to be". How true those words are. My experience left me with no doubt in my mind and the minds of my family and many of my friends that we would never purchase a Mercedes-Benz again as my experience proves that they just do not value their customers anymore.

So far just from me Mercedes-Benz have lost over £250,000 in future purchases. What company today is willing to lose that amount, also losing future revenue from my friends and family who too would never again purchase a Mercedes-Benz. They also lose out on servicing, they lose.

Not only is their customer service shit, their vehicles are shit too.

Having a high degree of confidence affords me the comfort to defend myself in these unfortunate situations. As you develop your confidence you too will feel better able to defend and stand up for yourself when these situations arise.

DO NOT BLAME OTHERS

Unfortunately, and for the worst, we now live in a 'blame everyone else' society. People burn themselves on a hot cup of coffee and look to sue others for their own stupidity, always looking to blame everyone else for their own dysfunctional fucked-up life. As soon as Shit4Brainz wakes up and realises that the faults lie firmly within themselves they can now begin to make the effort to change and focus on creating their own happiness.

Sadly, there are those people who will never even accept that they are their very own fuck-up in life.

Yes, things will go wrong, things will fail. Who would you rather be, that lazy unhealthy individual sitting in their armchair watching daytime telly with the remains of last night's take-away evidently spilt down one's clothing with remote control in one hand and a can of beer in the other, moaning about just how bad life is and always will be, one of life's many losers – or would you rather be someone who is focused on being as happy

Creating your own Happiness

and successful as one possibly could be, willing to work hard and work hard at developing oneself?

I know which one I would rather be, and I know which one I choose to be. It sure has worked for me, because for every day I wake up, I am as happy as I can be. I have an amazing life, a life I created. I started with nothing, a violent father who beat me, who tried to instil into me that all I would do in life was sweep the streets.

Now I must stress a point here; even if I had become a street cleaner that is no bad thing, we require street cleaners, they do an excellent job, it is a job, they are working, earning a living. My father's words were pathetic; even when he was bellowing them at me at the very young age of five I knew that I was going to be successful, that I was not going to allow his negative approach to control the direction my life traversed in.

Even when he left my mum when I was ten years old, how happy that day was. I even helped him load his car but he still tried to control me, dictating to me that I must work in his business, drive a Japanese car because, as he stated, they were the best.

He also made it very clear that when I received my wages, I was to give them directly to him, so that he could decide just how much he felt I needed to see me through the week, and he would keep the rest. Yes, that is what kind of an evil bastard he was.

When I secured my job as a cabinet maker, on a Friday afternoon, the day I would be paid, he would wait outside of my workplace to take my wages from me. To combat this I would leave through the timber storeroom doors onto the next street and make my way home from there. No way was I going to allow him to control my life and my happiness.

I learned from a very young age how control works, be it by our corrupt government, religion or family. I was never going to be controlled. Being confident makes me solid, it allows me to create my own happiness, to establish my own set of rules, my own laws, I live my life my way.

POSITIVE THOUGHTS BRING POSITIVE RESULTS

In life you may be a worrier, certain things may bother you and play on your mind; well, we can all say at some point in our lives we have our problems and concerns. What could be referred to as my number one problem in life: people, always has been always will be. Yes, I have had my fair share of unreliable cars, unreliable pieces of technology, but by far the one thing in life that causes me more problems is people. Generally people are shit!

Yes, in my life people have caused me more problems, being unreliable, dishonest, fake, I could go on and on. You know what my attitude towards it all is: IT REALLY IS NOT WORTH ALL THE STRESS. My mindset is so strong, I do believe if you are a good communicator and have common sense you can pretty much work problems and differences out with most people and if you cannot, then just go your own separate way, simple as that.

My mother's wise words, 'There is always one', were so right. At school there was one, at Air Cadets there was one, in my first job when leaving school on a Youth Training Scheme in 1983 there was one, working at Thomas Pearson there was one, becoming a Stuntman ironically there were several, neighbours throughout the years: what am I referring to? Troublemakers. They are negative, jealous of you and your success, your lifestyle, the house you own, the car you choose to drive, your occupation, they are interfering troublemakers, the shit on my shoes. I am so pleased I do not have to live with the fuckers, can you imagine just how miserable their home life is? My home life is amazing and I structured it to be that way.

As you are aware, I keep my association with negative people to a minimum, always have, always will. I just do not have time for negativity in my life, it really is not worth all the stress. I have encountered my fair share of problems. I would not change one single thing if I could turn back the clock. I focus only on the better side of life; everything else is insignificant. I can handle any problem I am faced with and SO CAN YOU.

I have a technique I developed back in 1987 called 'reverse psychology' and it goes like this.

There is always one person, no matter what direction we take in life, who will become a problem if you allow them to. Working at Pearson's was no exception, and that person went by the name of Andy. Andy was also a cabinet maker, ten years older than I, with a very bad temper, who suffered mood swings just like a spoilt fourteen-year-old girl. I was able to deduce that if I did not stand up to this individual he would make my working life a misery. I was enjoying work so much I was not prepared to allow The Cock to ruin my day. I know how to play people, I am a master at it. Even as a sixteen-year-old I was astute enough to establish that Andy was a bully and was looking for his next punchbag. In his mind, I was just what he was waiting for.

I knew that squaring up to him was not going to resolve his attitude problem, as one day he could be very friendly then a few hours later be a right bastard. Time for reverse psychology. Andy had bought a Vauxhall Astra from a local dealership near his home in Loughborough which developed a radiator leak. Each morning he would arrive at work looking under his car to check that the leak had been repaired, he would then make some tea, venture outside with his morning drink and check his radiator again. Now the clever part. I mixed antifreeze and water into a spray bottle, so each morning when he arrived at work, religiously checking to make sure his radiator was not leaking, as soon as he entered the workshop, I would spray under his radiator to make it look as though his car was leaking again. There I would be in the yard, cutting some wood, as Andy would stroll out with his cup of tea, calling me a toerag, as he usually did – whatever that meant I never knew – then he would check his car.

This is the best bit: he would explode into a rage, a friggin' volcano erupting, charging into the boss's office to telephone the dealership to inform them that "My radiator is leaking again, you useless fuckers have not fixed it, I'm gonna kill every one of you!" For the rest of the day he would be checking his car, wondering why it was no longer leaking. Each morning I would repeat the process and Andy would erupt with anger, until he took his car in the following Saturday morning.

On Monday when he arrived, we would all be very cool and quiet then ask, "What happened about your car?" Andy would reply, "They checked it and said it was not leaking." None of us would answer, continuing with our work, until I found the ideal moment to spray his radiator again, then all hell would kick off. It was a true classic moment, Andy bursting through the doors, yelling, "The fucker is leaking again!" I tortured the bastard so much he eventually sold the car and bought a Reliant Robin.

That, my readers, is reverse psychology at its best.

In my many years of studying reverse psychology the most valuable lesson I have learned is not to ever lose one more sleepless night worrying over other people's minds. Just focus on your own mind, your own thoughts and focus on being the best person you can possibly be.

A recent conversation I had with a very good friend established a clear understanding that there is far more evil in this world than good, I am sorry to say; unfortunately my life's experiences have drawn me to this conclusion.

But for all the evil out there I am not going to allow it to affect my happiness, NO WAY.

IT'S ALRIGHT FOR SOME

I remember hearing these words many times, when I park up in my Lamborghini, meet with so-called friends I have not seen for some time, or just in passing meet an acquaintance I used to know from years gone by; they see the car I drive and their response is, "It's alright for some."

This makes me realise just how lazy and unmotivated people are when they say this. Do they really think that my Lamborghini dropped out of the sky with my home and all the other possessions I have worked so hard for? And I emphasise the word WORK, I have not won, inherited, found, stolen or been given anything in this life; I have earned every penny I have through my own dedication, courage and hard work and my very smart approach to finance. As you know, I have developed the Midas Touch.

There are many hardworking people out there trying to put food on the table for themselves and their families and I do understand at times people become unemployed. This in life can come to the hardest of workers through redundancy or even ill health. There are those people out there who shy away from a good day's work, sponge off the state, leeching wealth from our corrupt government like our unnecessary parasitical Royal Family, what a complete waste and a drain on this country they are and the sooner they are abolished the better. I was so disgusted at our corrupt Police Farce arresting members of Republic at the crowning of 'super parasite' Charles, whatever the fuck he is calling himself this week. Vagina, that it prompted me to join Republic, and also my fiancée bought me a copy of a great book entitled Abolish The Monarchy by Graham Smith.

What many people forget is that The People have the power, NOT our corrupt 'Shit4 Brainz' government. Confidence gives you POWER!

Remember to hold your head up high, be proud of what you have achieved and be happy. Never bow down to those who look at you with jealousy. Be polite to them by all means, but as I have many times stated, keep your association with these individuals to an absolute minimum. Let Losers associate with Losers, they are just the shit on your shoes and will always remain that way.

Happiness is a state of mind, think happy and you will be happy, think sad and you will be sad. It is just how our minds work. Focus strongly on being as happy as you can possibly be, do not bother with other people's thoughts and negative opinions of you, like I have said, THEY DO NOT MATTER. Find the things in life that make you truly happy and concentrate on those as much as is practicably possible.

It may be raining outside, and yes we all can sometimes feel low when the sun does not shine. Tomorrow is another day, look at life in a positive way, if it bothers you that much that you live in a country that has shite weather, bad unemployment, in your mind no great future, you can always look at the option of moving abroad, this is an option so many people take each year and never look back. Do remember, you could still encounter the same shite you are experiencing now only the sun will be shining.

During my time since becoming a Stuntman in 1993 I have encountered regular negativity from my colleagues; I just do not expect any better of them. What I do not do is to allow it to bother me. They can be as negative as they like, all doom and gloom, it won't work, it will fail, baling out copious volumes of shite which reflect just what their personality represents, Negativity.

It did make me wonder about their life, upbringing and outlook that, having the best job in the world that they were still not happy. As Stuntman we get paid handsomely; however I must stress that because of the law of supply and demand producers are pushing down rates and certain Stuntman are willing to sell their sorry ass for a pound note. I was able to deduce that no matter what, they would never be happy, and this trend is synonymous throughout mankind, not everyone is positive, not everyone has the ability to think in a productive way: that can be changed only if the individual is willing. If not their life will always stagnate.

As you are aware, I had a purely evil father: he was violent, abusive and negative. Now in life as we develop through childhood, we have what is referred to as learned behaviour. Ironically, I was smart enough even as a very young child to establish that my father's behaviour was toxic, and that I was NOT going to allow it to have a negative impact on my future. I established my FUEL FOR MY FIRE approach from a very young age, determined to prove him wrong and that not only I would be successful, but that my intention was to be super successful.

There are always other ways, other options, it is up to you to look for them, put some thought into your life and do not and never say, if I had X it would make me happy, because if that is how your mind works believe me you will never be happy, NEVER.

When I was growing up I had very little but I was still happy; when I left school and was earning £25 per week on a Youth Training Scheme I was happy; was I satisfied? No, absolutely not. My ambition is a very strong driver, I strive to be the best I possibly can be; I work SMART, I work HARD. I knew there was more, and I had the dedication to progress and that is exactly what I did, from my taking up Kung-Fu to training to become a Stuntman. I knew it would take hard work, I was prepared and it paid off.

I have the amazing life I enjoy for one reason and one reason only, ME. I was hungry for success, I MADE IT HAPPEN!

Are you hungry? Are you hungry enough to work HARD and better yourself?

Now the reading of this chapter is complete I want you to do something for yourself: as you are aware at the end of each of my chapters, to help and guide you I include helpful pointers.

At the end of this chapter I shall not do this. You will. As you are aware, this chapter is focused on you and your happiness. Now write down all the things that make your life happy. I now want you to make a conscious effort to do some or all of the things you have written down, do something now that makes you happy, do something next week that makes you happy and most of all do something that will benefit someone else and make them happy and I can guarantee you this, that smile on their face will make you content.

KEEP SMILING.

CHAPTER 14

DRESSED FOR SUCCESS

What makes a person successful? Success can be measured in several ways. Some people judge an individual's success by the way they dress, the car they drive, by the home they live in, without really getting to know the person deeply enough to be able to assess just how successful someone really is.

I do not believe for one second that the success of a person is measured by wealth. If you have completed my book, absorbed the information and are now putting your reading into practice to make your life much happier and more productive, it could be said that you have now become successful in your goal to become more confident.

You may not have great ambitions, you may just want to be the best person you possibly can be, you may want to work hard to give yourself the best chance in life so that you can look back and say, "Yes I have been successful in cultivating a rewarding future."

SET YOUR GOALS

Throughout my life I have always been ambitious. In 1988 I started to set yearly goals; at the beginning of 1988 I decided I was going to take up Kung-Fu that year and I did. The rewards I have from that experience will remain with me for life; as you are aware, that experience changed my life and changed my life for the better.

I realised that if I set a goal at the beginning of each year and worked hard towards accomplishing what I aimed to do, I always was successful in achieving my desire. To this very day, I have continued this tradition, having achieved so much which I am very proud of. If I venture further back to the day in 1987 when I saw the Ferrari and Porsche 911 Cabriolet

I was hungry for success. That is the problem with today's youth, they are not hungry enough.

In 2000 I was featured in The Guinness Book of Records as The World's Most Versatile Stuntman doubling for a height range from 3'6" right through to 6'4", that is, every height in increments of one inch. Now that is some achievement for a guy who stands at 5'3" tall.

I have trained in Shaolin Kung-Fu constantly to date, achieving my Eighth Dan Shaolin Red Sash this summer of 2024 which I am so proud of.

My amazing stunt career can be seen on my website www.fallingforyou.tv.

And if you ever need any inspiration just look at what I have achieved and that is some going for a guy who came from the back streets of Nottingham. I believed in myself, I invested in myself, it paid off as hard work always does. That is what having confidence does, it gives you the motivation to know you can and will succeed.

Lazy bastards need NOT apply!

GREAT RECOGNITION

There has never been a place in my life for modesty. I strongly believe that if you are good at something then say you are good and if people do not like you for it and call you big-headed and full of yourself, so what? Just ignore them.

They say what they say because through their own insecurities they are jealous, they do not have the confidence to fulfil their ambitions, basically they are lazy, remember our friend who sits watching shite time television, far too lazy to get off their sorry ass and better their life.

I have never been one to hold back my words, as you have noticed. I have achieved so much in my life, and I am proud of every achievement, award and recognition I have rightfully deserved. A very proud moment for me

With Confidence

was when I discovered that I had been featured in Jamie X Oliver's (not the chef) fantastic book Secret of My Success. Jamie interviewed me back in 2007 for the Daily Telegraph newspaper. After several years of interviewing top business leaders Jamie decided to write a book, compiling all the features of the successful businesspeople he had interviewed.

I was very proud when opening Secret of My Success and witnessing my name, alongside business greats like Richard Branson and Bill Gates.

I am not afraid to show off my success, we were born to shine and I shine. Jealousy is worse than cancer; cancer can be cured, jealousy cannot. I grew up with nothing, Mum did her very best to give my brother and me everything she possibly could so that we survived, and what I mean by survived is that we had only just enough to live. We did not receive pocket money, we very rarely were bought toys, I was happier drawing shapes in a muddy puddle with a stick than playing with expensive gifts. My bastard of a so-called father left Mum in Shit Street, leaving for another woman.

No one will ever penetrate my armour. I made myself successful, I have every right to show off, I earned that right through hard work, bravery and courage, do you know what? You can too, you can have the most amazing life possible, or you can hide away because you are scared, you are a coward and afraid to stand out just in case you might upset someone.

Back in 1983 when on a Youth Training Scheme I could guess which students were going nowhere fast; they were troublemakers, disruptive and not willing to learn.

There was one individual who dedicated his time to making my life a misery. If he had dedicated the same volume of time into learning to be a bricklayer he would have become a great success. However his bullying was having an effect on me. I was 16 and he was 16 but I only looked 10 and was not very strong, as at this point in my life I had not yet started Kung-Fu. If I had I would have kicked seven shades of shit out of him.

He was a troublemaker, a bully and as we are aware bullies are cowards. This very day I was 'dressed for success'; by that I mean I was prepared.

We were mixing mortar for our brick laying course. "Shit4Brainz" was his usual troublesome self, trying to fuck up my day; enough was enough, I was going to fuck him up for life. We mixed mortar on boards and our teacher would come over and check it. On this particular day, "Shit4Brainz" decided he had issues with my mix. Interesting, as I had issues with his personality which resulted in my missing my mortar and smashing hard down on his shin with my shovel. Ho, silly me, never saw him again, PROBLEM SOLVED!

HARD WORK PAYS OFF

Being appreciated is a great reward in itself; unfortunately, in life it does not happen that often, as some people would much rather put you down than praise you for your efforts. I am very proud of what I have achieved. I am very proud of my home; I love my house very much and I love the work I have done to make my home life comfortable and luxurious. Anyone entering my home will see several photographs of me in action on many of the television and film productions I have worked on. I am proud to display my work.

Some people for strange reasons have shown disapproval at seeing these photographs decorate my walls. I can only presume that through their own insecurity, lack of talent and most of all jealousy that they find what I am so proud of offensive. Fuck em! Well that is simply their problem and if that is all they have to complain about in life then they are very fortunate.

No room for modesty in my life as you are aware, I personally believe modesty gets you nowhere. Be proud of who you are, be proud of what you have achieved, work hard, save hard, train hard and you too will become successful and be able to enjoy your efforts for many years to come, and most of all help others, and never forget this, as one day you may need someone's help too.

SO YOU WANNA BE SUCCESSFUL?

So what exactly do you want to do? What exactly do you want to achieve? You know from earlier reading I focused on MAKE YOUR PLAN. I firmly believe to be successful, to have that confidence that you so desire, you really need to know what you wish to achieve. Without a plan you are going nowhere fast. It is pointless getting into your car and not having a clue where you are going, you need to know what you aspire to do or become.

I remember walking into a friend's study and witnessing hundreds of Post It notes stuck all over the walls, on the back of the door, all around the frame of the windows, and written on each Post It note was his goal, wish, ambition, not just to make himself rich and successful, also to make himself a much better person.

These notes fascinated me. I began to read some of them and was able to assess what kind of mindset he had. He wanted to stop letting people down, he wanted to become more reliable, he wanted to stop being late, he wanted to earn lots of money, be adored, there were so many things he wanted to do and his way of hoping that he would achieve them was to expose himself to what he considered to be all his faults, his aim was to be able to remove a Post It note when he was happy that he had made good and positive progress in that direction.

I looked at what he had done as a very honest way for a person to expose themselves to what they consider to be their faults; most of what he had written were more about what he felt he needed to do rather than what he wanted to achieve. Admittedly he was a very lazy person, he suffered that disease by the name of jealousy. I remember the day I told him I was training to become a Stuntman. After he had pissed himself laughing, he said I would never make it. What he was actually saying was that HE would never make it, if he desired that kind of goal. He was useless, what was interesting was that he hoped that by writing his aims down that they would just happen without effort. Life just does not work that way. You HAVE TO WORK HARD, YOU HAVE TO MAKE THE EFFORT. If you are not prepared to do this, then you have already failed.

THE LACK OF CONFIDENCE

How many times have you said to someone, I am going to do a bungee jump, skydive, run a marathon, sail around the world on a bread board, ask that pretty girl out, and their reply is, "No you won't." When someone attempts to knock you back with the words, no you won't, what they are actually saying is, no, they would not have the courage or confidence to do what you wish to achieve. I experienced this so much earlier on in life, but I never suffer negativity towards me anymore as I never have to prove myself.

I have experienced this attitude many times in my life. I do not ever experience it now that I am a professional Stuntman, as there is no doubt in anyone's mind just how much courage and drive I now have to achieve anything I set my mind to.

Even back in my school days whatever I said I wished to do I was always hit with the reply "No you won't." In 1983 we were talking about work; the fact that England was in recession did not mean anything to me because I did not even know what a recession was. What I did know was that I would land a job, no matter what: however, my classmates thought differently, with the attitude that 'you will sign on like the rest of us'. Did I sign on like the rest of them? No, I disciplined myself to find a job and that is exactly what I did.

(Just to make those who have never heard the term 'signing on' aware, signing on was a process for an unemployed person to receive benefits.)

When I started cabinet making, as you are aware I worked with the most miserable and negative people you could ever meet, all doom and gloom. It did not matter what I said I wanted to achieve, it was always met with 'no you won't'. I have said it before and I will say it again and I will keep saying it, WE ARE ALL DIFFERENT.

Throughout my life I have experienced many knockbacks as you are aware; you may have or will too. Sit with a group of people and say to them, "I want to be an astronaut" and see what their reactions will be. Now just think of it this way. Several people throughout history have said these very words and have become just that. Many people have said they wish to be self-employed, set up their own business, and that is exactly what they are doing now. Anything is possible if you have the drive to succeed. You have to be hungry and not only hungry, you will have to ignore the negativity that will inevitably come your way.

Each and every one of us can achieve exactly what we wish. The reason that not everyone grasps their goal is that through simple human nature most people are lazy and will always give up, which gives you that added advantage that they will drop out of the race and you will keep running. No matter what the weather I train, I never miss my training unless I am on-set working or I am ill, nothing else will prevent me from training, no excuses, I train. Same with my business, when I became a Stuntman I established 'Falling For You'. I am a businessman, a very successful one at that. I dedicate the time 'Falling For You' requires, I make time to write, it takes a considerable volume of time to write a book, I make time, NO EXCUSES, I DO IT!

YOU KNOW THE SAYING

You can take a horse to water, but you cannot make it drink. Read that line again, now think about it, how true it is, you can give a person all the tools and help they need to make them a much better person, to make them successful, to help them develop their confidence; however, if they are not thirsty enough to drink you are wasting your time.

I have tried to help several people, I have sat down with them, explained to them what they need to do, I have even given out free copies of my book to try to help them, no longer. I have found that the people I give a free book to never read it and why? Because they do not appreciate it, simple as that, because they have not used their own money they have worked for, they place no value on what they have before them.

IT WILL NEVER HAPPEN AGAIN

I will never give a book out for free to anyone who needs a good hard kick up the ass, because that is exactly what a great number of people need to get themselves motivated.

The kind of people I am referring to are those individuals who sit there feeling sorry for themselves saying, "I wish life was better." Well, get off your fat lazy ass and make it better. Some people really think they have problems, when what they really need is a wake-up call. They need to be exposed to real hardship. There are some people on this planet as you read these very words I type, who do not even know where the next meal is going to come from. There are people out there right now, not knowing where they are going to lay their heads to get a good night's sleep, that is if they are even able to get a good night's sleep. There are many people in this world who are suffering abuse and real hardship. Some people really do need a wake-up call so they can realise just how fortunate they really are.

HELP EACH OTHER

You could never read this far into my book and not have progressed in a positive manner, with your mindset changing all the time. As you read my words of value, you have become more confident, happy, positive; however, have you become more caring? I really do hope so.

There are many qualities that you can take from my writing that will make your life more rewarding and fulfilling, and what better way of rewarding your life than by rewarding other people's lives too. Help people and never be afraid to ask for help too. I really feel that not enough people help each other. There is far too much greed in this world, far too many people only thinking of themselves, are you thinking what I am thinking? MPs; not you, Nigel.

I have an aim for you just for today but do not be afraid to practise this thought every day. I want you now, today, to help someone in whatever way you feel you can. It does not have to be anything great or grand, just do something that will help someone, something that will put a smile on your face and on the face of others, see how it makes you feel after knowing that you have made someone that little bit happier and made someone feel a little more valued.

My parents brought my brother and I up to always have good manners. Yes, my father had his faults, don't we all. My parents brought my brother and I up to be polite and good-mannered, and still to this day and until the last nail is driven into my coffin I will always be the polite good-mannered gentleman that I am.

Whatever you wish for, whatever you want to achieve, anything, absolutely anything is possible, only you are holding yourself back. Take those barriers down and see just how happy and rewarding your life will become, keep those barriers in place and your life and the life of those close to you will suffer.

ENJOY THE NEW YOU

Be very proud of yourself, for you have taken time from your busy life to better yourself. You have been the one who has looked at yourself and your life and have decided enough is enough, I do not want to carry on anymore being used and not chasing my dream. For every minute you have dedicated to reading my book you have become confident in yourself and your beliefs. For now your mind thinks in a positive and constructive manner. You are now thinking less of negative events in your life and more looking positively towards your future.

Do remember that no matter what negative events happen in your life, and they will, there will always be a positive hiding somewhere. Life at times can be shite; I have experienced my fair share of bad times throughout my life. I used to say, "Why did this have to happen to me?" I never say that anymore, I accept what has happened and I look for any lessons I can learn, I look at ways to improve my situation, then I move on, I do not dwell anymore. Shit happens!

Look back at the motivation you once lacked. No one read this book for you. It has taken a considerable amount of motivation for you to dedicate the time required to make the effort to read. From this day forward you will keep becoming stronger and stronger and yes, you will experience problems; as you are now well aware, being confident will not make you immune to any form of problem or emotional upheaval throughout your life. Your ability to deal with any negativity which may come your way will never be a problem in your life for very long, as long as you follow my philosophy and DO NOT allow anyone to control your happiness and future.

WORDS OF WISDOM

Whatever direction you decide to take in life, whatever road your life takes you along, there are many things you will be grateful for and amongst them will be your newly developed confidence.

Be very proud of yourself. For no amount of money in this world can ever buy you what you have developed. Your confidence will now stay with you for the remainder of your life, helping you to become a strong, healthy and successful person, most of all allowing you to be what we all aspire to be.

HAPPY.

WHEN YOU CAN ACCEPT FAILURES, MISTAKES AND PROBLEMS

WALK AWAY WITH A CLEAR MIND

DILUTE ALL NEGATIVE THOUGHTS

CHANNEL YOUR ENERGY INTO POSITIVE THINKING

YOU HAVE ACHIEVED THE ULTIMATE

PERFECT CONFIDENCE

www.ingramcontent.com/pod-product-compliance
Lightning Source LLC
Chambersburg PA
CBHW020356170426
43200CB00005B/192